Mastering Digital Librarianship

Strategy, networking and discovery in academic libraries

Mastering Digital Librarianship

Strategy, networking and discovery in academic libraries

Edited by
Alison Mackenzie
and **Lindsey Martin**

f facet publishing

© This compilation: Alison Mackenzie and Lindsey Martin 2014
The chapters: the contributors 2014

Published by Facet Publishing,
7 Ridgmount Street, London WC1E 7AE
www.facetpublishing.co.uk

Facet Publishing is wholly owned by CILIP: the Chartered Institute of Library
and Information Professionals.

British Library Cataloguing in Publication Data
A catalogue record for this book is available from the British Library.

ISBN 978-1-85604-943-6

First published 2014

Text printed on FSC accredited material.

MIX
Paper from
responsible sources
FSC   FSC® C013604
www.fsc.org

Typeset from editors' files by Flagholme Publishing Services in 10/14pt Palatino
Linotype and Frutiger
Printed and made in Great Britain by CPI Group (UK) Ltd, Croydon, CR0 4YY.

Contents

Contributors

Jill Benn is Associate Director of Research and Learning Support in Information Services at the University of Western Australia, one of the Group of Eight research intensive universities in Australia and ranked in the top 100 universities in 2012 in the Shanghai Jiao Tong Academic Ranking of World Universities. Information Services is a converged service which encompasses information technology support and services, library and information services as well as audiovisual facilities and support. Jill is responsible for library and IT services at the six subject libraries on campus, including reference and information literacy services. Jill has presented papers at a number of national and international conferences and has over 10 years of experience in the development, delivery and management of reference and information services.

Contact Jill by email: jill.benn@uwa.edu.au

Moira Bent is a Faculty Librarian at Newcastle University and a National Teaching Fellow [HEA, 2005]. Her research interests are focused around information literacy, facilitating research, transition into HE and international student support. As well as publishing several journal articles and book chapters, she is co-author of the SCONUL Seven Pillars of Information Literacy, Core and Research lenses (2011), Vitae's Informed Researcher (2012), *Providing Effective Library Services for Research* (Facet, 2007) and SCONUL's Guidelines on Library Services for International Students (2008). Amongst other responsibilities she chairs the UK Universities Science Librarians' group, is a member of the RIDLs Coalition (2012) and is a reviewer for the i3 International Programme Committee, the LILAC Conference and the Journal of Information Literacy.

See Moira's blog: www.moirabent.blogspot.co.uk

Rachel Bury is an Academic Liaison Manager within Learning Services at Edge Hill University, Lancashire, UK. Learning Services provides a range of complementary academic services, including library services and learner support, comprising IT, academic literacies and support for students with a specific learning difficulty (SpLD); and learning technology and media development teams who provide support and expertise on technologies to support teaching, learning and research to academic staff, students and researchers. Her current role involves overall responsibility for quality and marketing and communications, including managing the Learning Services web presence, working with collaborative library partners and statistics.

Rachel received her degree in Library and Information Studies from Manchester Metropolitan University. She has worked in higher education since 1999 when she was appointed as the library manager for Edge Hill's health sciences library on the Aintree Hospitals NHS Trust site, Liverpool. She had previously worked as an NHS librarian managing a postgraduate medical library for seven years and, previous to that, in public libraries in Manchester. More recent management and strategic roles have focused more on academic liaison and engagement, information literacy and marketing and communication.

Contact Rachel by email: rachel.bury@edgehill.ac.uk
or follow her on Twitter: @rachelriding

Lisa Charnock is the Marketing and Communications Officer at Mimas, The University of Manchester, where she works across a variety of services and innovations projects to co-ordinate activities such as market research and user evaluation, events and exhibitions, and copywriting. She is particularly interested in user research, and works with colleagues across Mimas to help them gain a better understanding of the needs of our user communities.

Lisa has worked in higher education for over 15 years. Before joining Mimas, she worked as an academic liaison librarian at Edge Hill University Library, where her main focus was helping students and academic researchers to discover and make the best use of information and resources. Through her work with Mimas she has developed a strong interest in how the web and emerging technologies are changing the way we research and use information.

Joy Davidson is Associate Director of the Jisc-funded Digital Curation Centre (DCC). She is also currently Principal Investigator for the Jisc-funded Data Management Skills Support Initiative – Assessment, Benchmarking and Classification (DaMSSI-ABC) project, and is also a partner in the EC-funded Collaboration to Clarify the Costs of Curation (4C) project. She is involved in several international working groups including the Knowledge Exchange Primary Research Data Working Group and the Research Information and Digital Literacies Coalition (RIDLs).

Alison Hicks is the Romance Language Librarian at the University of Colorado, Boulder. After graduating from the University of St Andrews, Scotland with an MA in French and Spanish, Alison worked in Buenos Aires, Argentina before completing her MSIS from the University of Texas, Austin. After a brief stint in Washington, DC as the Public Services Librarian at the Inter-American Development Bank, she moved to Colorado in 2008 where she is the liaison to the departments of French, Italian, Spanish, Portuguese and Comparative Literature. She also plays an active role in building connections and situating the librarian at the heart of various local communities through a variety of digital and physical methods.

As a tenure track librarian, Alison's work has been published in Communications in Information Literacy, Reference Services Review, Collaborative Librarianship, RUSQ and Portal. Her interests include the integration of critical information literacies into foreign language learning, changing digital scholarship practices, and building community through participatory culture. Originally from Somerset, UK, she is fluent in French and Spanish and is happiest when she has her walking boots on.

See Alison's URL: http://alisonhicks.weebly.com

Helen Howard is Skills@Library Team Leader at the University of Leeds. Her role involves managing the Skills@Library service which promotes academic skills development in students by providing workshops, online learning resources and 1 to 1 advice, as well as support for academic staff. She works across the University to ensure students are offered high quality and timely support to develop a broad range of academic skills to enhance their learning, research and future employability. Prior to her current role, Helen has worked at Leeds University Library in different roles since 1996, providing a range of support for students, researchers and academic staff. She has been a member of the SCONUL Working Group on Information Literacy and is a Fellow of the Higher Education Academy.

Helen is interested in the blend of information literacy with a wider set of academic skills to provide a holistic approach to student skills development. Her interest in digital literacy skills development led her to co-author the SCONUL Seven Pillars of Information Literacy, Digital Literacy lens. She has written a number of articles and given various presentations on these two themes in particular. She is also a member of the CoPILOT committee, a UK group promoting the sharing of information literacy teaching and learning materials as open educational resources.

Contact Helen by email: h.e.howard@leeds.ac.uk

Helen Jamieson is Customer Services Manager within Learning Services at Edge Hill University, Lancashire, UK. Her current role involves overall responsibility for the libraries' learning spaces as well as managing and developing all physical and virtual enquiry services. Helen has worked in Higher Education since graduating in 1997 and has worked in libraries for the past 15 years. Roles have been varied and have included document supply, developing services for distance learners and delivering learner support. More recent management roles have focused more on operational and strategic responsibilities in relation to learning spaces and service provision. A particular interest for Helen is the area of customer service and she is the service lead for Customer Service Excellence award, which is an award issued by the UK government for excellence in customer service.

Contact Helen by email: helen.jamieson@edgehill.ac.uk
or follow her on Twitter: @JamiesonHelenA

Alison Mackenzie is the Dean of Learning Services at Edge Hill University. Prior to taking up this post, she held the post of University Librarian at Bangor University, Wales, had a variety of roles at Manchester Metropolitan University and in her early career worked in art colleges and commercial practice.

Alison has been active in SCONUL for a number of years, as a member and Chair of the Working Group on Information Literacy and as a contributor to the e-learning task-and-finish group. She has been active in the promotion of digital literacies and is currently managing a project on behalf of SCONUL on the development of digital scholarship skills by information professionals. She is currently Chair of the Performance Measurement and Quality strategy group and is co-editor of this book.

Contact Alison by email: alison.mackenzie@edgehill.ac.uk

Lindsey Martin is the Assistant Head of learning Services at Edge Hill University, responsible for the learning technologies managed and supported by Learning Services. She has overall responsibility for the virtual learning environment and its associated systems, media development, classroom AV and ICT support and ICT staff development. Lindsey has worked in academic libraries for the past 19 years in a variety of roles including liaison librarian, research co-ordinator and manager of SOLSTICE, Edge Hill's HEFCE funded Centre of Excellence for Teaching and Learning. She first became involved with e-learning as an academic librarian creating e-learning modules to support colleagues and students developing information and digital literacies.

Lindsey is a member of the editorial board for the *SCONUL Focus* journal and secretary of the Heads of eLearning Forum Steering group (HeLF), http://w01.helfcms.wf.ulcc.ac.uk/. She is co-editor of this book.

Contact Lindsey by email: Lindsey.Martin@edgehill.ac.uk
or follow her on Twitter: @lindseymartin

Dawn McLoughlin is the Associate Director, Resources and Development at the University of Western Australia. Her role includes responsibility for information resources access and discovery, human resources and finance and the University's eResearch and Digital Developments Unit. Dawn joined UWA in 2012 and prior to that worked in the UK at Edge Hill University as Academic Support Manager for 10 years. This role encompassed responsibility for academic liaison, academic skills support, support for students with a specific learning difficulty and ICT training within a converged library, IT, media and online learning service. Dawn has presented at a number of national (UK) and international conferences.

Contact Dawn by email: dawn.mcloughlin@uwa.edu.au

Julie Mitchell is the Managing Librarian for the Chapman Learning Commons at the University of British Columbia in Vancouver, Canada. In her role, she provides leadership and management for all areas of learning commons operations and works collaboratively with the campus community to develop learning support and academic enhancement opportunities for students, both physically and virtually. Based in the Irving K. Barber Learning Centre (IKBLC), Julie also contributes to the planning and development of IKBLC's learning spaces, particularly in support of student programs and services. Passionate about teaching, learning, and innovative applications of new technology in the library environment, Julie is interested in empowering students to become successful lifelong learners.

Dr Kay Munro is a College Librarian at the University of Glasgow Library, providing support to the College of Social Science. She has a particular interest in the impact of technology in libraries. She has a key role in a number of Library projects looking at particular aspects of emerging communications and information technology developments. These include the implementation of the Library's mobile technologies strategy, the development of a more user-focused website and social media presence, and the development of a Library game, which it is hoped will add the social and fun elements of gaming into interactions with the Library for its users. Kay has co-published a number of articles and papers relating to mobile technology initiatives at the University of Glasgow Library.

Contact Kay by email: kay.munro@glasgow.ac.uk
or follow her on Twitter: @kayjmunro

Joy Palmer is the Senior Manager for National Library and Archival Services at Mimas, The University of Manchester. She is responsible for the strategic direction of services such as Copac and the Archives Hub, for securing funding, and for designing and overseeing related innovations projects in areas such as resource discovery, analytics and digital humanities. She also heads up Mimas' marketing and user-research activity.

Joy earned her PhD in English Literature in 2005 and taught across a wide range of subject areas and different levels from first year to advanced undergraduate. She joined Matrix, a Digital Humanities Centre based at Michigan State University in 1999, where she gained a breadth of experience in developing grant-funded, multimedia-education and research projects. She is interested in how the web not only changes models of information consumption, but alters the very way in which we 'know' or experience the world, and her work looks at the role of web technologies in changing approaches to content creation, mediation and reuse. She remains involved in digital humanities, working with colleagues at The University of Manchester to explore the potential of working with new technologies and large-scale data sets to evoke and encourage new research questions.

Rosemary Stenson is Head of Information Resources Services at the University of Glasgow Library, with particular responsibility for cataloguing policy. Rosemary convenes a number of Library Groups working on various aspects of both the mobile technology and evidence base strategies and has been heavily involved in the continuing development of the search and discovery services. She has co-published a number of articles and papers relating to mobile technology initiatives at the University of Glasgow Library.

Contact Rosemary by email: rosemary.stenson@glasgow.ac.uk

Karen Stevenson works within the Digital Library Team at the University of Glasgow Library. She is the Library Management System Co-ordinator and also focuses on usability of the Library's search and discovery services. Karen has been a member of the Library's Mobile Technology Group since it was established in 2010 and takes a key role in aspects relating to training and skills development in the mobile environment. She has co-published a number of articles and papers relating to mobile technology initiatives at the University of Glasgow Library.

Contact Karen by email: karen.stevenson@glasgow.ac.uk

Cindy Underhill is a Strategist, Learning Resource Design, within the Centre for Teaching and Learning Professional Development at the University of British Columbia in Vancouver. In her current role Cindy is engaged in a variety of projects related to the development of web-based resources to support learners. She is interested in the application of social web approaches to support learning – wherever it happens. Cindy has been a college instructor, considers herself a learner, is proud to be an amateur at most things and has been involved with educational technology and distance learning for the past several years at UBC. She shares work-in-progress and the occasional observation about learning (mostly) on her blog Potentially Coherent at http://cindyu.wordpress.com/.

Contact Cindy by email: cindy.underhill@ubc.ca

Wendy Walker is Head of Metadata Services at the University of Glasgow Library and her responsibilities include the management and promotion of the Library's non-serial e-resources collections. Wendy is the Vice Chair of the Ebook Group of SCOPNet, the procurement activity for the Scottish Confederation of University and Research Libraries (SCURL), and has been actively involved in ensuring that access via mobile devices is a key priority. As a member of the University of Glasgow Library Mobile Technologies Group she co-ordinates the activities relating to the testing of access to content via a wide range of mobile devices. She has co-published a number of articles and papers relating to mobile technology initiatives at the University of Glasgow Library.

Contact Wendy by email: wendy.walker@glasgow.ac.uk

Introduction

Alison Mackenzie and Lindsey Martin

What is academic librarianship when it is no longer characterized by the traditional practices of cataloguing, acquisitions, content management and committee attendance? Much has been achieved over the past two decades by harnessing technology to advance the availability of content and to better streamline and navigate access to resources. New learning environments have also emerged to facilitate academic activity and considerable investment has been made to extend and introduce new communication choices for users of library services. But are these by themselves achieving a level of mastery of the digital environment which will secure a role for the profession of librarianship into the future? Is there a need to accept that the future gains from continuing to identify library-related uses for the internet are diminishing and that new approaches to librarianship should be sought?

Lorcan Dempsey (2012) suggests that if librarians want to be seen as experts, then their expertise has to be visible. He makes a number of observations – is library expertise visible when people are searching? Can they easily discover a personal contact? How should librarians position themselves to attract attention from other professional networks? Are they seen as natural supporters, partners and collaborators? How are libraries positioned to engage with emerging social and professional networks?

The American College and Research Libraries (ACRL)[1] planning and review committee, in its 2012 top ten trends in academic libraries, both endorses and expands on Dempsey's observations, further confirming that libraries and librarians need to be engaged in identifying more effective approaches to communicating their value, curating and preserving digital resources, forging new partnerships both within and beyond institutional boundaries and adapting their services to meet the expectations of new generations of users. Alongside many admirable and successful initiatives, some of which are discussed in this book, a turning point has been reached where some of the traditional measures of value for an academic library no longer hold the relevance or importance they once had. What is now tasking many librarians is the identification of new measures of success and how these can be achieved and made visible.

One challenge to achieving this is that 'too many librarians see their collections, not the community, as their jobs' (Lankes, 2012). He proposes that librarians and library practice need to build on the understanding that knowledge is created through conversations with their communities. Following on from this, libraries need to structure their services and identify their priorities around their communities, finding out through discourse and conversation what is expected. These conversations need to be embedded in daily practice and as this practice evolves, what is currently regarded as perhaps innovative, or novel, will over time become the expected, not the exceptional. New services may emerge from these conversations and flourish or fall victim to the transient nature of digital fashions and rapidly fade. This is indicative of the transient nature of technologies, a view supported by the annual EDUCAUSE Horizon report,[2] which only forecasts up to four to five years in the future and identifies that timescale as 'long term'. Librarians need to consider how they can best thrive in this environment of exponential change. By maintaining close contact not only with their communities, but also with other professional groups both inside and beyond their own institution, they will be in a better position to deliver the best of their professional expertise. This supports Dempsey's analysis of the importance of visibility to the success of the library and that marketing, networking and communication have to be afforded the appropriate levels of attention and investment.

This book offers an honest appraisal by academic librarians of their professional practices at a point in their transition. Based on insights by librarians into their working environments and what they consider to be vital for the success of their careers, their services and their profession, it demonstrates a surge of creatively informed decision-making, challenging some of the practices that have traditionally characterized the profession. Broadly divided into three themes, the foci are on practices which illustrate the importance of communication and marketing activities; the professional expertise required to support new academic practices; and the opportunities and challenges of delivering resources in a digitally rich environment. Many of the initiatives are using technologies as vehicles for creation, consumption or both, but in all cases success is not ascribed to the technologies, but the opportunities they offer to librarians to design new services.

A thread which weaves through many of the contributors' chapters is the recognition that success is dependent on acquiring a clear understanding of what is required by the customer base. What we are learning is that using social media for 'telling and selling' services and collections to library users is only skimming the surface of its potential – and in some cases media are being abandoned for lack of uptake. Harnessing the power of social media requires libraries to rethink their whole approach to marketing – adopting a strategic, customer-centred approach which goes far beyond using Facebook and Twitter for promotional activities. These new conversations are using social media to engage at a granular level with different customer groups encouraging new relationships, based on personalized, not generic, contact.

Hicks draws her inspiration from Lankes' (2011) use of social media to better understand and engage with her library community in the online spaces they inhabit, bringing in effect the library to the user. Her approach to the use of digital media to communicate with customers is a means to an end and not an end in itself. She believes that her role is about forging relationships with library users, not simply promoting the collections. This belief informs many of her activities as she explores how to maximize her contributions as a subject specialist and librarian.

Using technology to enhance individual enquiry services was the focus of research undertaken by McLoughlin and Benn, whose survey of university libraries in Australia confirmed the view that technologies which enable personalization are more likely to be successful. They also draw attention to the need to consider different models for enquiry support, which reflects a growing sophistication of choice by their user communities.

The importance of investment in marketing and communication is illustrated by the growing number of appointments which specifically address these areas for strategic development. In contrast to earlier appointments, whose remit may have been associated with a specific aspect of a service, e.g. special collections, new appointments appear to have a much wider remit. One of the challenges for those appointed to these roles is to ensure there is a shared understanding amongst senior managers that internal marketing is crucial in creating a customer-centred marketing culture. Bury and Jamieson discuss the importance of this within the broader context of strategic priorities for library services, highlighting the importance of marketing and how the value(s) associated with promotional campaigns can have a significant impact on the trusted status of the service within its user communities.

The second series of chapters focuses on three key communities of users – academic staff, researchers and students – and how libraries and librarians can provide the required expertise and support to maximize effectiveness when working with open content and research data. There are clear opportunities for librarians to grow and broaden their roles in supporting digital literacy, open educational resources (OERs) and research but there are also challenges arising from lack of awareness, confidence or engagement. The final chapter in this section reflects on how one library service has extended students' digital capabilities, working in partnership with other professional services to identify the opportunities and the pitfalls of operating within an open digital environment.

One recurring theme present across all chapters, but directly relevant to the success or otherwise of these new activities, is the development of new partnerships. In some instances these will evolve organically and over time become established; others are born out of a strategic necessity where there is a clear recognition that success is dependent on collaboration. With both models the potential for tension exists, arising from conflicting priorities, differing cultures and working patterns. The danger is that, if not addressed at an early stage and a negotiated outcome reached, problems may arise downstream with an impact on schedules, progress and ultimately success. These challenges will be familiar to many, but what has also emerged from observations is the hidden cost associated with partnership working; working collaboratively with students involves training time, staff resources and materials; working with other professional groups within a university may be unfamiliar and time spent agreeing the 'rules of engagement' may impact on progress.

However, the rewards in many instances outweigh the initial barriers, including in most instances cost. There is now an extensive body of literature which details the desirability of multi-professional teams and it is in the interests of libraries and librarians, as Dempsey observes, to be seen as 'natural supporters, partners and collaborators'.

Howard in her chapter focuses on the evolving role of librarians' support for and use of open and digital content. Developments and engagement by librarians in this area provide a superb example of where some of the traditional practices are adapted to meet the needs of the digital environment; expert advice and guidance on intellectual property rights (IPR) and copyright for open content; support for staff and students on the production, use and deposit of OERs; and staff training and development. These are all activities which extend the traditional role of the librarian into new arenas while still retaining the integrity and specialism associated with the profession.

The extension of the role of librarian into new areas is also discussed by Davidson, who draws attention to how the librarian can become a key player amongst a range of contributors to the processes underpinning research data management. Success of institutional strategies is clearly dependent on multi-skilled teams, working collaboratively in various combinations dependent on the needs of specific activities. Again, this shines a light on the role of librarians and how and where they position themselves to attract attention from other professional networks as well as initiating conversations with the right people.

Students as partners are a key focus of the chapter by Mitchell and Underhill, whose project the Digital Tattoo combines the skills of librarians in developing and supporting digital literacies and applies their expertise to assist students on the formation of their digital identities. It identifies the strength that partnership working brings and highlights the importance of a participatory culture to the success of the project.

The final section of the book deals with strategies designed to maximize access to, and delivery of, resources and services. It provides examples of where librarians have responded to the challenges presented by the uptake in mobile and other technologies and have developed innovative practices to enhance and extend customer services and improve access to resources.

Munro and colleagues at the University of Glasgow discuss their approach to the development of a mobile library strategy. Customers sit at the heart of their strategy and their behaviours inform priorities for investment, support and development. This ongoing engagement with their user communities helps to keep the strategy on track and limits the risks of derailment or poor investment.

A key priority for academic libraries is to demonstrate that the investment made in resources delivers an acceptable return – this is traditionally captured by tracking usage but many reporting tools only capture a limited view of the data. A recent project is exploring how circulation data can be used to track student reading habits and, using the activity data, to provide alternative reading recommendations. This is work in progress, but the findings as discussed by Charnock and Palmer suggest that use of this data may release currently untapped potential, bringing to the surface material which is not immediately visible but will provide readers with suitable alternative recommendations to their original search.

The final chapter in the section provides a case study for the provision of a library service to an overseas campus. Alongside detailing some of the specifics associated with delivering a virtual service, Bent draws attention to early engagement by the library in the university planning process; the importance of working with other professional partners at the home and overseas campuses; and the advantages which accompany opportunities to supplement the virtual with face-to-face interaction. At all times the needs of students and staff sit at the heart of decision-making and this is amplified when negotiating across cultural and language boundaries:

> In a world where attraction and return on attention – defined as the value gained relative to the time and attention invested – are becoming increasingly important, those who master the techniques required to shape serendipity will likely profit far more than those who simply wait for it to surface.
>
> Hagel III, Seely Brown and Davison, L. (2010), 98-9

The view of Hagel et al. suggests that a higher productivity yield is achieved when the following are seen as strategic priorities:

- choosing environments that increase our likelihood of encountering people who share our passions
- becoming and staying visible to the people who matter most
- influencing their endeavours so they amplify our own
- discovering and influencing the right people at the right time (timeliness)
- making the most of every serendipitous encounter (relevance).

This strategic approach signals a significant shift of emphasis; its fluidity and perceived lack of clear objectives may feel uncomfortable but the potential gains in establishing and building new partnerships and networks, digital and face-to-face, to progress developments provide compelling reasons for testing the theory.

This is not to say that traditional approaches to service development are uniformly redundant. There is an ongoing need to evaluate the success of all practices and although not a topic discussed in detail here, the growth of interest in, and attention paid to, performance indicators to help inform decisions, in particular those based on qualitative feedback, is indicative of the preparedness of librarians to more readily adapt, adopt and retire services in response to customer needs.

As Hagel and his co-authors observe, 'pull is not a spectator sport', and the contributors to this book exemplify the gains to be achieved when using their influence, expertise and communication skills to forge new partnerships, to explore and deliver new services and to enable their communities to achieve their academic and research goals.

Notes

1   http://crln.acrl.org/content/73/6/311.full.
2   http://net.educause.edu/ir/library/pdf/HR2013.pdf.

References

Dempsey, L. (2012) Some Modest Notes about an Informational Future. In Marchionini, G. and Moran, B. B. (eds), *Informational Professionals 2050: educational possibilities and pathways*, School of Information and Library Science, University of North Carolina at Chapel Hill, NC, http://sils.unc.edu/sites/default/files/publications/Information-Professionals-2050.pdf.

Hagel III, J., Seely Brown, J. and Davison, L. (2010) *The Power of Pull: how small moves, smartly made, can set big things in motion*, Basic Books, New York, NY.

Lankes, R. D. (2011) *The Atlas of New Librarianship*, MIT Press, Cambridge, MA.

Lankes, R.D. (2012) *Expect More: demanding better libraries for today's complex world*, North Charleston, SC, CreateSpace.

THEME 1

Rethinking marketing and communication

CHAPTER 1

Digital marketing in an outreach context

Alison Hicks

Introduction

Marketing or public relations has a chequered history in libraries. For cautious administrators, it represents a perilous minefield of potential legal challenges to the university's brand and image. For others, it is one step closer to the corporatization of libraries, on a level with coffee shops and outsourcing cataloguing. Even for libraries that have set up a Facebook page, marketing can often be seen as slightly creepy or slightly inane; a waste of time that diverts staff and resources from the library's decreasing budget. Notwithstanding, a 'library's collection and services are relevant only to the extent that they are used by their intended audience' (Smith, 2011, 333). In an increasingly complex information environment, marketing, or the promotion of products and services, is key.

Digital marketing, which refers to the use of digital technology for promotion and outreach, has often been seen as adapted to new undergraduate internet lifestyles and a way to promote the library's higher-quality online information resources (Smith, 2011, 334). However, just as 'smartphones are not just miniature PCs' but possess their own ecosystem, digital marketing cannot be seen as a direct extension of traditional library marketing activities (Aldrich, 2010). Instead, it is important that libraries examine the wider social and cultural effects of technological change, as well as new tools, in order to design authentic and effective outreach and marketing strategies.

Accordingly, this chapter will provide an overview of digital marketing and outreach in the LIS context, looking in particular at the experiences of academic libraries. Drawing on the work of David Lankes, it will take a broad approach to the library's role in the changing information landscape, effectively situating new tools and techniques within the movement towards user-centred librarianship. Within this framework, the chapter will highlight overarching themes from this outreach model, while also focusing on examples of general tools such as Twitter, mobile or location-based tools such as Foursquare and visual tools such as Pinterest. The bulk of the chapter will consider the benefits, issues and impact of this process and will provide examples from the aforementioned tools to illustrate major points. The chapter will finish with a series of questions that are derived from the University of Colorado, Boulder (UCB) experience and designed to help the planning process.

From marketing to outreach

In 1999, a simple website called the Cluetrain Manifesto exploded onto the scene (Locke et al., 1999). Published just before the dotcom bubble burst, its 95 theses, or manifesto, provided an early and prescient glimpse of how the internet could affect people and organizations. Over a decade later, its central premise that the internet has enabled a 'powerful global conversation' remains key. As the authors predicted, the rise of networked media has facilitated much broader two-way communication, which, in turn, has required a radically new response from organizations. It took over ten years for this vision to be translated into the context of librarianship, but in 2011 David Lankes published *The Atlas of New Librarianship*. Just as in the Cluetrain Manifesto, Lankes' vision of libraries and librarians of the future understands the need to focus on these conversations. For him, librarians have become overly focused on the products or the artefacts of knowledge such as books. He makes the case that instead librarians need to concentrate on facilitating the conversations that are at the heart of knowledge creation. As such, his vision focuses on the need for librarians to understand and engage with the local community, a return to the core principles of librarianship.

By subtly challenging the purpose and focus of libraries, Lankes opens the door to re-examining the objectives of many library activities and services, as well as librarian attitudes and actions. The concept of marketing proves to be no exception. If librarianship is about facilitating knowledge creation in the community, then it is clear that unlike traditional marketing, online engagement is not just a vehicle for delivering services or promoting a product. Instead, the purpose of digital marketing must be to reach out and engage this community, to understand its needs and to create an environment that will facilitate and connect patrons to knowledge-creating conversations. By focusing on the relationships in a community rather than the transactions, digital marketing brings the library to the user, thereby enabling a true sense of participation and ownership of the knowledge creation process (Lankes, 2012).

It is not just the goals of digital marketing that are adjusting to a networked world. Libraries have a great deal of expertise as well as valuable collections and services to offer online communities; credibility is one of our biggest assets (Lankes, 2011, 92). Yet none of this matters if a library cannot connect with people online and become part of their community and conversation. Therefore, libraries must also change the way that they communicate in online settings. This can be summed up as the need to listen, both to what users want as well as listening for feedback; to be authentic, or to respond to user needs in a human or genuine manner, rather than sounding soulless or defensive; and to share or to participate in online communities, ensuring librarians form part of changing digital spaces and habits (King, 2012). David Lee King refers to this as 'sounding human on the web' and it is a vital part of digital marketing (King, 2012, 1).

In sum, digital marketing is not just about translating traditional marketing online, or keeping up with new online tools. Instead, it involves engaging authentically with the new spaces, tools and voices that form the community's online conversations, focusing on the way that the librarian can engage, understand and build relationships with community members. For many, the change in focus has been so wide-reaching that even the term marketing appears inadequate to describe the additional advocacy, outreach, community engagement, promotion and advertising involved (Ford, 2009). While a broader discussion about terminology does not fall within the scope of this chapter, what is key is that librarians are talking about the importance of digital marketing and outreach within their communities, a process that should be widespread and ongoing.

In practice

Accordingly, together, both Lankes and the Cluetrain Manifesto provide a firm theoretical basis and model for digital marketing and outreach in the academic library. On a more practical note, however, it is important to realize that digital marketing presents its own set of challenges as well as benefits to the community. It also has a wide impact on users, staff and library services. As such, the following section will attempt to explore these areas while referring to three types of outreach tools: general tools such as Twitter, mobile or location-based tools such as Foursquare and visual tools such as Pinterest. Recognizing that digital marketing is not defined by technology (as well as understanding the fluctuating nature of the social media environment), this chapter will not give a step-by-step introduction to individual tools. Instead, a basic overview of major categories or types of tools and their affordances will be provided to situate the reader, while the recommendations for further reading will provide examples of practical tips.

There are a variety of different tools that can greatly expand and streamline the digital marketing process. Tools that will be referred to in this chapter include the following.

General outreach tools, e.g. Twitter

These comprise well known and established tools that already have many functions in community and individuals' lives, such as socializing, networking and information sharing. Twitter and Facebook are the major tools in this category, though Google Plus is also gaining ground as more universities adopt Google Apps for Education. Already embedded in many people's lives, these tools are indispensable for a wide variety of functions in the library: for example, sharing practical or real-time information such as hours changes or closures, asking opinions through polls, sharing photos of new services, books or librarians, hosting virtual book groups and more. For more ideas see Sump-Crethar (2012); Phillips (2011); and Forrestal (2011).

Mobile or location-based tools, e.g. Foursquare

Drawing on the ubiquity and popularity of mobile devices as well as social gaming, these tools develop the concept of library as place, as well as helping to study library usage. One of the biggest tools in this category is Foursquare, a mobile application that allows users to 'check in' to places that they visit, thereby informing friends of their location and providing recommendations of local amenities (see Figure 1.1). Well used on US campuses, Foursquare allows users to claim prizes when checking in to a place, including badges, or the title of 'Mayor' if they are the person who checks in most frequently at a specific location. As such, Foursquare can be extremely useful as a type of loyalty card, offering special deals for the Mayor or users who check in a certain number of times as well as highlighting library services via tips and to-do lists. For more ideas see Vecchione and Mellinger (2012).

Figure 1.1   *Example of UCB Foursquare account*
Source: Alison Hicks, University of Boulder, Colorado

Visual tools, e.g. Pinterest

The newest category of digital outreach tools, visual content curation tools, are ideal for promoting library collections, particularly images of physical or digitized collections. Pinterest, which is similar to HistoryPin, is a way of gathering images from the web in one place to create an online scrapbook or inspiration board (see Figure 1.2). Users can then see or re-share these images with friends and contacts. Forming part of the move towards online content curation, or the gathering and the presentation of content around a specific topic, these tools can be used to provide a visual promotion of library collections, for example, new book covers or reading lists, or to enable wider use and sharing of library images, such as digitized photos of local collections. For more ideas see Dudenhoffer (2012) and Thornton (2012).

Benefits

What are the identified gains to a library that engages with digital marketing? This section will look at four of the major benefits to libraries and librarians, which can be summed up as building relationships, gaining feedback, widening the impact of the library and staff professional development.

Figure 1.2   *Example of New York Public Library Pinterest account*
Source: Alison Hicks, University of Boulder, Colorado

Building relationships

As David Lankes points out, the ability to build relationships with local community members is one of the major benefits of digital marketing. For Phillips (2011), this is because establishing relationships with students not only increases the possibilities of regular library interaction, but also establishes the library as a trusted resource that goes beyond a provider of books. In addition, she believes academic libraries are ideally positioned to bond with these students because 'the university context creates a strong foundation of shared experiences, history and culture for academic libraries and students' which the library can reinforce via digital marketing (Phillips, 2011, 519). Nevertheless, these relationships are not automatic. In online social networks, interpersonal relationships must be built on trust and credibility to build rapport between students and organizations. To build the user's trust, though, the library must be perceived as relevant and approachable. As such, digital marketing must be used to tell the story of the library's multifaceted identity. Not only will this improve the library's social capital, but it will also expand user knowledge of library services (improve relevance) as well as demonstrating library support for the community, including the shared local contexts (improve approachability). It is only then that users can see the library as a credible resource in their network and feel safe exploring the research environment.

While building relationships is important for increasing usage of librarian and library services, it is not an automatic process. Furthermore, it is highly dependent on librarian interactions. As such, it is important that librarians

Figure 1.3
Example of a serious tweet
Source: Alison Hicks, University of Boulder, Colorado

Figure 1.4
Example of a playful tweet
Source: Alison Hicks, University of Boulder, Colorado

are not afraid to engage people online. As Sump-Crethar (2012, 353) says, 'users want to interact with people, not buildings', and accordingly, librarians should act as authentically as possible with patrons. At the University of Colorado, Boulder (UCB), librarians actively look for opportunities to follow and engage with self-identified UCB students as well as other UCB campus groups, to build this sense of shared community. This can be through doing a search for people who use the phrase University of Colorado Boulder (or derivations) in their profiles, or more gradually by following people who mention the library. In addition, Twitter uses a recom-mender system to suggest other accounts to follow, meaning the more relevant people the library follows, the more visible the account becomes.

People who staff the services are encouraged to adopt a casual tone that acknowledges the student's milieu, while also remaining aware of professional responsibilities and the library's academic support role. This could be characterized, perhaps, as similar to an aunt–niece relationship rather than mother–daughter; the library is playful without being too censorious, while also knowing when to draw the line (see Figure 1.3 for an example of serious tweet and Figure 1.4 for an example of a less serious tweet). Librarians who are uncomfortable with online identities should take some time to immerse themselves in the online chatter before attempting to post or interact. Laura Solomon (2011) has some good tips on how to develop an online voice, as well as improve postings.

Feedback

The second main advantage of using general or location-based digital marketing is the ability to gain feedback on current services from library users. One way this can be achieved is through administering polls and surveys, for example to Twitter or Facebook followers. It can also be done by studying user data, such as the in-depth Foursquare reports that detail use and demographic statistics among others. In turn, being able to analyse this feedback for insight into library or service usage enables librarians to become far more responsive to user needs. Ethnography, a research design that captures cultural habits, is becoming core for many libraries in their quest to design spaces and services that are based around users. Digital marketing tools that are used in an ethnographic manner can help build detailed pictures of user habits and ensure even basic decisions are user-driven. At UCB, a series of polls about popular magazines helped librarians select new material for the Learning Commons. Equally, use statistics from Foursquare enabled librarians to make more informed judgements about opening hours.

Tools such as Twitter can also be used to find out what users are saying about a library or a service. At UCB, a proximity keyword search in Twitter for the library's name, or the word 'library', used within a 15-mile radius of Boulder, caught many insightful comments about the library. These comments lead to greater insight into the problems users were experiencing with the library, for example a lack of power outlets and study tables. It also lead to increased possibilities of interaction and relationship building within the community, for example by being able to reply to complaints and show patrons that the library was actively working to improve services.

Widening impact

The third main advantage of digital marketing tools is that by their very nature they enable wide sharing among many different individuals and communities. This means that digital marketing can broaden the scope and impact of libraries among a much more dispersed audience. One of the obvious examples is increased recognition and knowledge of small local or niche collections. By sharing local digitized collections on content curation tools such as Pinterest, for example, libraries can easily situate themselves as key hubs in certain areas of local history or genealogy, thereby helping to build more important relationships within their community. Libraries can also use these digital tools to tap into and take advantage of the wider network of interest on a topic. In 2008, for example, the Library of Congress allowed Flickr users to add tags and additional information to almost 5000 photos. Nearly 70,000 tags were added (and only 25 were inappropriate), thereby greatly expanding the use and impact of their collections (West, 2008).

Digital marketing can also help extend library services beyond traditional barriers, for example among users who may not know about or use the physical library. This means digital marketing may introduce the concept of library services to new patrons or decrease library anxiety by repackaging traditional library content into a familiar environment, for example a Facebook page (Dickson and Holley, 2010, 14). In this way, as the information landscape fragments even further, digital marketing enables librarians to bring the library to the users, even if they were unaware of traditional library services offered. Digital marketing can also be used to join the physical and virtual library together. Many library communities will include people and groups that may only be active online, or that may not realize that the online library has a physical counterpart (and vice versa.) And, as Wisniewski (2010, 55) points out, the separation between online and physical resources often leads to a lower-quality user experience of the library. For example, online help pages are rarely embedded at the point of need in the physical world. More poignantly, he argues that librarians spend a great deal of time, effort and money purchasing online resources such as databases and that simple business sense indicates that librarians should maximize these expenditures in the physical world too (Wisniewski, 2010, 55). Digital marketing can help bridge these worlds. Foursquare and other location tools (as well as other ideas such as QR codes) provide a good example of patrons using online games to find what the library has to offer physically as well as virtually.

Lastly, as more and more communities are creating knowledge uniquely or predominantly online, social media is playing a bigger role than ever in non-traditional spaces such as digital scholarship, or embedded librarianship. As the academic world starts to use Twitter, for example, for networking and information-sharing practices, digital marketing provides a way for libraries to establish themselves as a hub or contact in the online network, thus ensuring that librarian expertise is still accessible even as scholarship starts moving from individual offices to collaborative online networks. Ellen Hampton Filgo provides a good example of this in practice when she embedded herself in a class Twitter account, serving as a resource throughout the semester (Young, 2011).

Professional development

Finally, digital marketing, especially using social media tools, is useful for librarians' professional development. Librarians who use tools for outreach will also be improving their own personal learning, networking and information-sharing habits. The information world moves very quickly and familiarity with these tools is important to ensure that librarians remain connected and anticipate change. Furthermore, as social media plays an increasingly important role in digital scholarship, online engagement will be key for academic librarians. In this way, both the library and the library staff can benefit from increased familiarity with tools and the information environment.

Issues

Despite the benefits, digital marketing is not without its issues or problems. These can be summed up as problems with authority, questions about the value of digital marketing, copyright and information storage.

Authority

One of the biggest challenges to digital marketing may be overcoming internal or wider resistance to establishing a digital presence. Inside the library, staff may not see the benefits of social media, or be wary of 'pandering' to non-traditional library use, especially as other demands on librarian time grow. Equally, managers and the IT department may not be keen to relinquish control of social media around the library, or may insist on rigid rules or limits. Marketing librarians may feel threatened by the need to give other members of the organization a voice. Outside the library, the university may have strict rules designed to protect the image of the college, especially in today's brand-conscious environment.

While digital marketing could leave the library open to attack or criticism, libraries with appropriate social media policies are well placed to deal maturely with any problems that may arise. After all, if the library is being mentioned online, then being able to respond with the library's point of view is key. Librarians have traditionally represented the library at the research desk and should be trusted to make judgements for social media, too. While staff should be aware of potential pitfalls and the need for appropriate tone and actions, these potential problems should not be allowed to stop experimentation.

The UCB Twitter account was initially established as a six-month pilot project. A group of library faculty presented a detailed planning document that outlined goals, proposed activities, assessment and time management. Passwords and log-in details were also shared among administrators. In addition, staff drew up a set of recommendations for appropriate online interactions. After this was (reluctantly) approved, the evaluative report detailing feedback and evidence of interactions more than demonstrated the importance of the account to outreach and the library has not looked back since. In addition, in over two years the library has not experienced any incidence of online malicious behaviour. UCB also highlighted their participation in the campus-wide social media group to allay university administrators' fears. This ensures that the library accounts meet existing rules but also means that librarians can help craft appropriate new regulations.

Value

For many, the value or 'return-on-investment' of social media and digital outreach remains questionable, both in terms of mission creep and rates of usage, as well as the cost of staff time and library resources. Firstly, as library budgets decrease, social media marketing can be seen to sap a lot of valuable staff time. Even though tools are mostly free or have a very low cost, social media marketing must be proactive; responding to users must be timely and both posting and monitoring for feedback needs daily attention. Libraries must also keep up to date with changes in the field, including checking for changes within tools (e.g. new privacy settings) or new tools completely. It also takes time and planning to keep track of where everything is posted and ensure that the library's message remains consistent yet personalized across many different types of tools. Secondly, usage of social media may be low, or may be used primarily by those who are not members of the library's community. For example, Abby Bedford (2012) estimated that on average, 48% of library Twitter followers are not affiliated with the primary library community. It may seem that a lot of effort is being expended in return for very little visible change, for example increased visits to the library. In addition, assessment information about digital marketing is often anecdotal or vague and there has been little statistical analysis of effectiveness (Dickson and Holley, 2010, 11). Lastly, for many librarians, digital media may seem superfluous to the library's mission, taking time and energy away from traditional or more important library duties.

To meet these challenges, it is important that libraries assess their community needs and consider the purpose of their digital marketing before signing up for accounts. For a start, certain tools may not be right for every community; in a tightly knit community, for example, there may be less dependence on general social media tools. Adequate initial assessment can help ensure that staff time is not wasted. When UCB first started investigating location tools, the library opened accounts with Foursquare, Gowalla, Facebook Places and Google Places (some of which are now defunct). Careful examination revealed that Foursquare was by far the most popular, which led to a focus on that service. Similarly, it is important that digital marketing is assessed as part of the library's wider marketing strategy rather than on its own. Libraries should also make sure to follow campus constituents, rather than celebrities or even other libraries or librarians. This will help ensure the account has more appropriate or targeted visibility through recommended user systems, too.

Lastly, a structure to support social media implementation will help ease many of these problems. For Troy Swanson, this is not a social media plan, which implies a rigidity that will not work in the organic, evolving social media landscape (Swanson, 2012b). Instead, Swanson encourages libraries to create a safe environment where library staff can experiment with social media, as well as setting out basic policies, workflows, guidelines and best practices to encourage participation. This may also help overcome administrator caution or fears. Depending on how the service grows, a co-ordinator may be necessary to streamline outreach; making social media an integral part of a staff member's job will help promote the value of this work. Nevertheless, participation from many voices in the library will help spread the workload, while allowing a variety of staff to experience how useful digital marketing can be. At UCB, five self-selected, interested librarians staff the Twitter service regularly. Thematic or topical calendar planning helps streamline the day-to-day processes, thereby reducing overlap or duplication. For example, in Week 1, all tweets will cover finding reserves/short-loan books, finding textbooks at the library, maps, etc. Librarians agree to try and post twice a week on this topic as well as other related topics that arise, e.g. news events or literary birthdays. Other libraries assign librarians specific days to post. In addition, two of the five librarians gather and collate feedback in a shared Google Doc for distribution to managers each semester. It is, however, important to strike a balance between planning and action. While planning is key to overcome some objections or constraints, librarians should not overplan until they become paralysed by indecision or too many rules.

Copyright

Copyright is a key consideration when using new online tools. Pinterest, especially, has been accused of not respecting copyright laws by linking to images without providing citation details. While measures have been put in place to try and enable more ethical use of online images (Dudenhoffer, 2012), it is important that staff are aware of basic image copyright and that all images that are re-pinned from the library's account are cited with a link back to the original image. In addition, it is important that the library makes clear what the copyright terms are for any images that the library makes available.

Information storage

A final potential issue is that new information collected, for example, through tags or user comments on Historypin, or even interactions on Twitter or Facebook, is not easily captured or archived. As such, the information remains isolated and 'separate from the formal systems supporting the organization's collection' (Burford, 2012, 232). Similarly, it may be hard to extract data from programs if the library decides to switch platforms. Many of these problems remain insoluble. However, libraries should read terms and conditions carefully and endeavour to choose software that makes clear reference to ownership and moving of data. If librarians think valuable data could be gathered on a specific project or topic then initial planning should establish norms and procedures for archiving.

Impact

Now that we have studied the gains and the issues involved with digital marketing, what is the impact on library users, on staff and on library services as a whole? This section will examine the effects of digital marketing on these groups or areas.

Users

Digital marketing is a field in flux and as such, the impact on users is hard to gauge. Many early digital marketing studies were sceptical of library participation in social media, for example, worrying that librarians could be seen as imposing their academic authority into a student's personal online space (Dickson and Holley, 2010, 11). The phrase 'creepy treehouse' was even coined to describe this problem (Feldstein, 2008). Even now, librarians still worry about the fine line between outreach and privacy; for example, if a student that the library does not follow mentions the library on Twitter is it appropriate to respond? As social media becomes more prevalent, though, users have become more accepting of companies and professors using social media for marketing and educational purposes. In addition, most social media tools are public by default, meaning that users should be prepared for interventions. As long as the library's tone is professional and respectful, then it should not be too problematic. In fact, many people have praised the way that the UCB Libraries Twitter account has picked up on and responded to comments about the library.

Staff

The impact of digital media on staff will probably be fairly high. Social media is timely and needs a proactive approach. As such, staff need to have time to be able to participate. Staff training may also be needed, depending on existing levels of comfort. In addition, marketing can no longer be considered one person or department's job. Everyone must be prepared to speak for the library, as it is the wide mix of voices that helps the library sound human and connect with more users. While an outreach or marketing co-ordinator may be needed to co-ordinate passwords, schedules, marketing materials, poll prizes and more, it is clear that outreach needs to start to be embedded in every librarian's job, which again may take time or training. Subject specialists have a key role to play here, as the example of Ellen Hampton Filgo (Hamilton, 2012a) shows. Opportunities may exist for subject specialists to become even further embedded in their departments and communities of practice via social media and digital marketing. As such, additional conversations about the key goals and mission of the library may be needed as staff have to choose how to focus their time and energy. Lastly, the increased focus on local collections may require extra staffing or development of digitization and preservation efforts.

Services

Depending on the community needs and the number of the digital marketing strategies that a library decides to implement, the impact on services may vary. In some scenarios, digital marketing may enable the library to play a role in a completely new arena, for example digital scholarship, thereby expanding library service considerably. Digital marketing may also affect how librarians approach existing services, for example recognizing the importance of incorporating assessment and feedback into the provision of service. As such, digital marketing may help libraries move towards more user-driven and user-centred services, or understand the importance of ceding control to the community. The need to move quickly within the fluctuating social media environment may also contribute to creating more of a 'beta' attitude, where librarians are free to experiment with new ideas quickly and in a low-stakes situation without having to overplan.

Lastly, and perhaps slightly unexpectedly, digital marketing may enable greater clarity and focus on local or physical collections and services. As more general research moves online and digital marketing ensures the library plays a greater role in collaborative online scholarship networks, the role of the physical library can be more consistently defined as a hub for activities that are not always possible online, such as studying, face-to-face meetings, events or technical support; a makerspace (Hamilton, 2012b). As such, the physical library becomes more of a destination, the centre of face-to-face support and collaborative activity that complements the online library, just as in the successful Apple stores (Johnson, 2011). Digital marketing that establishes the library's role in the online research world, as well as location-based tools or QR codes that join the physical and virtual, will help develop the different roles of the online and physical libraries as well as ensuring greater connection between the two, thereby creating a more useful and enriching research experience.

Conclusion

In conclusion, digital marketing is dynamic and essential for libraries today. As research communities migrate online, digital marketing will help a library establish a presence in these new spaces, while also widening the impact of librarian expertise and service. Digital marketing is also essential as the library redevelops physical services to meet changing research needs and as a tool to gather feedback and assessment data during the process. While there are many stumbling blocks, to both the establishment and the maintenance of digital marketing, adequate planning should minimize the impact on overstretched library services. This is not to say that planning can anticipate every potential issue. In fact, the biggest challenge for librarians and libraries may be recognizing that 'disruption is a feature, not a bug' (Naughton, 2012).

Libraries are key in today's information landscape. By re-examining traditional practice within technological, societal and cultural shifts, it is evident that librarians' critical expertise remains essential – and that digital marketing can help establish this role. These changes do not mean that libraries should forget their past, though. For instance, even though librarians may borrow and adapt ideas from the corporate world of social media, it is vital that this is not at the expense of the library's core social values (Elmborg, 2011). In sum, forming part of the wider movement towards participatory librarianship that is centred around digital scholarship, user experience and ethnographic study, there is an 'expanding universe' of opportunity for librarians today (Gavia Libraria, 2012). In the case of digital marketing, this is the chance to use dynamic outreach opportunities to integrate core values into the changing information landscape. Let the conversation begin!

Appendix: Planning

Before any library undertakes digital marketing and outreach, it is important that appropriate planning is undertaken to guide implementation and maintenance of a service. The following questions derived from the UCB experience may help guide this planning. Also see Swanson (2012a).

1   **Study community:** What tools are already being used in your community? What are people doing online? Are there other salient characteristics, for example a high or low number of internet-enabled phones or devices? How could librarians or libraries help? What is missing from current online communities?
2   **Establish goals:** What does the service hope to achieve? In what timeframe? How will you know whether it is successful?
3   **Choose tools:** Which tools will you use? Who will keep the passwords? What do you need to get authorized as the 'owner' or manager of a location or account name? Are there any wider university guidelines that are applicable for the library? How will you set up the 'about us' page, including images, logos, brand? Will you push content from one central place? Or do you also need to set up other management tools such as Hootsuite or Tweetdeck? What about programmes to schedule tweets in advance, e.g. Twuffer? Which program will you use to shorten URLs? How will you maintain consistency across platforms?
4   **Staffing:** Who will post to the account? Will you do this all year or just

during semester? What about holiday cover? What training do staff
need? What about continuity if people leave or their jobs change? How
will you encourage a wide range of people to post? How will you get
dissenters on board?

5 **Posting:** Any guidelines for tone or type of material to be posted? How
frequently will you post? Will you make a topical calendar or allocate
people days of the week? Can you schedule certain tweets in advance?

6 **Community:** What is your policy on followers/friends? Will you build
this gradually or do targeted searches for followers? Does the
university maintain a list of campus groups that can be followed?

7 **Dealing with feedback:** Who will monitor for feedback? Who will
answer comments and suggestions? What will you do with this
information? What search words could you set up to catch mentions of
your library?

8 **Assessment:** How and when will you assess the service? What
qualitative and quantitative data can you gather and how will you do
this? What information do you need? What qualifies as success?

9 **Funding:** What prizes do you want for mayors, polls, surveys? How
will these be administered?

10 **Promotion**: How will this be integrated onto your webpage ('share this'
button, embedded feed, promotion of activity)? Will you promote around
the library? Around the university? In classes, posters, newspapers?

References

Aldrich, A. W. (2010) Universities and Libraries Move to the Mobile Web, *Educause Quarterly Magazine*, **33** (2).

Bedford, A. (2012) *Twitter: helpful or hassle?*, www.slideshare.net/bedforda.

Burford, S. (2012) Using Social Media in Information Practices. In Widen, G. and Holmberg, K., *Social Information Research*, Emerald Group, Bradford.

Dickson, A. and Holley, R. P. (2010) Social Networking in Academic Libraries: the possibilities and the concerns, *New Library World*, **111** (11/12), 468–79.

Dudenhoffer, C. (2012) Pin it! Pinterest as a library marketing and information literacy tool, *College & Research Libraries News*, **73** (6), 328–32.

Elmborg, J. K. (2011) Libraries as the Spaces Between Us, *Reference User Services Quarterly*, **50** (4), 338–50

Feldstein, M. (2008) The 'Creepy Treehouse', *e-Literate*, http://mfeldstein.com/the-creepy-treehouse.

Ford, E. (2009) Outreach is (un)Dead, *In the Library with the Lead Pipe*, www.inthelibrarywiththeleadpipe.org/2009/outreach-is-undead.

Forrestal, V. (2011) Making Twitter Work: a guide for the uninitiated, the skeptical and the pragmatic, *The Reference Librarian*, **52** (1), 146–51.

Gavia Libraria (2012) Steady-state vs Expanding-universe Librarianship, *Gavia Libraria*, http://gavialib.com/2012/07/steady-state-vs-expanding-universe-librarianship.

Hamilton, B. (2012a) Case Profile: Ellen Hampton Filgo, *Library Technology Reports*, **48** (2), 16-20.

Hamilton, B. (2012b) Makerspaces, Participatory Learning and Libraries, *The Unquiet Librarian*, http://theunquietlibrarian.wordpress.com/2012/06/28/makerspaces-participatory-learning-and-libraries.

Johnson, R. (2011) What I Learned Building the Apple Store, *Harvard Business Review Blog Network*, http://blogs.hbr.org/cs/2011/11/what_i_learned_building_the_ap.html.

King, D. L. (2012) *Face2Face: using Facebook, Twitter and other social media tools to create great customer connections*, CyberAge Books/Information Today, Inc., Medford, NJ.

Lankes, R. D. (2011) *The Atlas of New Librarianship*, MIT Press, Cambridge, MA.

Lankes, R. D. (2012) Community Outreach/Understanding Community Needs, *Virtual Dave . . . Real Blog*, http://quartz.syr.edu/blog/?p=1685.

Locke, C., Levine, R., Searls, D. and Weinberger, D. (1999) *The Cluetrain Manifesto*, www.cluetrain.com.

Naughton, J. (2012) *From Gutenberg to Zuckerberg: what you really need to know about the internet*, Quercus, London.

Phillips, N. K. (2011) Academic Library Use of Facebook: building relationships with students, *Journal of Academic Librarianship*, **37** (6), 512–22.

Smith, D. A. (2011) Strategic Marketing of Library Resources and Services, *College Undergraduate Libraries*, **18** (4), 333–49.

Solomon, L. (2011) *Doing Social Media So It Matters: a librarian's guide*, American Library Association, Chicago, IL.

Sump-Crethar, A. N. (2012) Making the Most of Twitter, *Reference Librarian*, **53** (4), 349–54.

Swanson, T. (2012a) *Managing Social Media in Libraries: finding collaboration, coordination and focus*, Chandos, Cambridge.

Swanson, T. (2012b) Your Library Does Not Need a Social Media Plan, *Tame the Web*, http://tametheweb.com/2012/12/11/your-library-does-not-need-a-social-media-plan.

Thornton, E. (2012) Is Your Academic Library Pinning? Academic libraries and

Pinterest, *Journal of Web Librarianship*, **6** (3), 164–75.

Vecchione, A. and Mellinger, M. (2012) Using Geolocation Apps for Academic Library Outreach and Instruction, *Reference Librarian*, **53** (4), 415–23.

West, J. (2008) Library of Congress Reports on Flickr Project, *Librarian.net*, www.librarian.net/stax/2607/library-of-congress-reports-on-flickr-project/.

Wisniewski, J. (2010) Bridging the Other Digital Divide, *Online*, **34** (5), 55–7.

Young, J. (2011) 'Embedded Librarian' on Twitter Served as Information Concierge for Class, *Wired Campus*, http://chronicle.com/blogs/wiredcampus/embedded-librarian-on-twitter-served-as-information-concierge-for-class/30000.

CHAPTER 2

Reference 2.0: evolution of virtual reference services and social media

Dawn McLoughlin and Jill Benn

Introduction

The emergence of digital technologies has provided significant opportunities for academic libraries to expand their service offerings. Technologies are now embedded in library services and almost all academic libraries across the globe offer some sort of digital enquiry service. These include free cloud-based services, such as Facebook and Twitter, as well as proprietary software and hardware hosted locally on a fee-for-service basis. This chapter offers an overview of the literature outlining the history of virtual reference, from e-mail systems to what is being described as Reference 2.0 using the current phenomenon of social media tools. Taking an Australian perspective, an institutional case study contextualizes the evolution of these services and is followed by an examination of the adoption of virtual reference services in Australian academic libraries. The chapter identifies some common Reference 2.0 success factors and offers a framework to assist in the choice, development and evaluation of new digital tools for enquiry services.

Literature review

As a considerable amount of literature exists on the use of technology in providing digital enquiry services within academic libraries, this review will focus on the history of virtual or digital reference and the mechanisms used for the evaluation of such tools.

From reference to Reference 1.0

Libraries began offering reference services in the mid to late 19th century, which became an established service in the 1890s (Fritch and Mandernack, 2001; Levinson, 1988). An early definition of reference work from this period is, 'the assistance given by the librarian to readers in acquainting them with the intricacies of the catalogue, in answering questions and in short, doing anything and everything in his power to facilitate access to the resources of the library' (Fritch and Mandernack, 2001, 288). This definition still applies in the present day; however, the introduction of new communication technologies has enhanced the provision of services.

According to Janes (2008, 8) there is no consensus on how to refer to the practice of electronic reference. Terms include digital reference, virtual reference, real-time reference, chat reference, live reference, and so on. For the purposes of this chapter we will refer to 'virtual reference', using the American Library Association (ALA) definition of 'a service initiated electronically . . . where patrons employ computers or other Internet tech-nology to communicate with reference staff, without being physically present' (American Library Association, 2004, 1).

Numerous studies have shown a decline in reference activity (Stevens, 2013; Aguilar et al., 2011; Jackson, 2002). Sidorko and Cmor (2012) report that the Association of Research Libraries Annual Statistics Service Trends show a 60% reduction in reference transactions over the period 2001–2010, with Australian academic libraries showing slightly less reduction over the same time period (49.5%). However, a number of studies reveal that 'though students may undervalue and underuse library resources and services, their research skills are unsophisticated and their ability to critically interact with the world of information around them is quite low-level' (Sidorko and Cmor, 2012, 3). This suggests a mandate for academic libraries to seek new ways of engaging with students to promote the value of library services and encourage the use of quality information. Online tools, particularly social media tools, afford an effective and efficient way in which this can be achieved.

Reference 1.0 emerged in the mid-1980s with the use of e-mail to receive enquiries and send responses (Janes, 2008; Arya and Mishra, 2011). After this came the use of web forms for question submission, with responses still provided by e-mail. This was followed by a range of synchronous, real-time technologies that were felt to be more akin to face-to-face reference interactions and included tools such as chat and instant messaging (IM). Chat technologies have been used to provide digital reference services since as far back as 1995 (Arya and Mishra, 2011, 150) and come in a variety of products, including free web-based services or proprietary software on an annual subscription basis.

Reference 2.0

More recently, library services have adopted a range of online tools defined as 'social networking' or 'social media tools' to deliver a different form of virtual reference, Reference 2.0:

> a reference service initiated electronically, often IM, co-browsing where users employ computers or other Internet technology to communicate with reference staff, without being physically present. Communication channels used frequently in virtual reference include blogs, Facebook, streaming media, folksonomies, videoconferencing, social networking software, tagging and social bookmarking   Arya and Mishra, 2011, 156

Although social media sites are not automatically regarded as digital reference tools, there is scope for them to become so, given their popularity and widespread use by university students. Indeed, Arya and Mishra (2011, 157) predict that 'Ultimately the Virtual Reference Service 2.0 model for service will replace out-dated, one directional service offerings that have characterized libraries for centuries'. Reference 2.0 is essentially causing reference services to shift from one-to-one reference interactions to a broader form of reference service with multiple, collaborative users.

The perceived benefits of social media for virtual reference include the ability to engage more frequently, easily and efficiently with users and the transition from one-directional reference to a more collaborative model. Additionally, users can contribute content and participate in answering enquiries submitted by other users. Tools coming under the banner of Virtual Reference 2.0 include Flickr, Facebook, LinkedIn, Del.icio.us, Twitter, Ning, Folksonomi, Instagram and MySpace. This review focuses upon Facebook and Twitter, as these are now well established and are particularly popular with the university student population for the opportunities they offer in the provision of collaborative reference services.

Facebook, Twitter and Reference 2.0

An analysis of *Times Higher Education*'s world's top 100 universities[1] (as at 2013) and the Shanghai Jiao Tong University's *Academic Ranking of World*

Universities [2] (as at 2012) found that 87% and 84% of libraries respectively had a Facebook presence. Use of Twitter is less popular but still relatively high, with 71% of university libraries having a Twitter account for both rankings. This supports the findings of Chu and Du (2012) and Hosny and Fatima (2012) and their assertions that libraries believe social media tools deliver value.

Facebook was, however, initially viewed with caution by the library sector. A 2007 Online Computer Library Centre (OCLC) report found that most of the US library directors surveyed did not see a role for social networking in libraries. It concluded that those surveyed

> believe that the library is for learning/information and do not see the connection with social networking and libraries. The general public saw social networks as personal/individual spaces and noted concerns about the library not knowing its community and issues of the library potentially exercising too much control. Librarians feel there are enough social networking sites existing already. Not unexpectedly, librarians also voice concerns about funding and resources
> De Rosa et al., 2007, 5–6

This view was reinforced by a survey of 126 US academic libraries which concluded that, 'While some librarians were excited about the possibilities of Facebook, the majority surveyed appeared to consider Facebook outside the purview of professional librarianship' (Charnigo and Barnett-Ellis, 2007, 23). Despite this, a number of authors, including Charnigo and Barnett-Ellis and Chad and Miller (2005) view social media as a valuable way to communicate with library users.

Reference 2.0 – a return on investment?

In a competitive environment where universities and sections within universities are vying for funding, academic libraries must demonstrate impact and return on investment in order to maintain or develop service provision. While there is a considerable amount of literature describing the use of digital reference tools and the benefits or pitfalls of their use, as well as literature from the early to mid 2000s on the evaluation of digital reference, there is little yet published on the evaluation of social media in a digital reference context.

Conyers and Payne advocate the importance of demonstrating value through evidence-based practice as follows:

Rather than relying on subjective impressions, libraries need to develop a robust evidence base to inform internal management decision-making and to support the management of change. Increasing sums are being spent by libraries on e-services and the digital infrastructure. Librarians need to know whether this represents good value-for-money as they are often making difficult choices between spending on new e-services and maintaining expenditure on traditional ones.   Conyers and Payne, 2011, 201

Conyers and Payne also highlight the importance of going beyond traditional statistical collection methods and surveys to demonstrate value and impact (which they argue is more difficult to collect and convey). They recommend service level agreements, aligning the library service more closely with the institution's own strategic aims and using a balanced scorecard approach to assist in determining impact.

The proliferation of academic library Facebook pages and the corresponding growth of discussion in library literature exists in contrast with the 'void [that] exists in the lack of reliable metrics, which we can use to assess the strength of our Facebook pages and their "return on investment" for our libraries' (Glazer, 2012, 18). Glazer recommends strategies such as having a stated purpose and setting appropriate goals, measuring 'fans', 'likes' and comments and seeking positive anecdotes in determining the impact of Facebook. Glazer also recommends a series of measures for boosting impact, including the importance of being interesting as well as interested, running competitions with prizes and talking about things other than your library (Glazer, 2012, 21).

While there is a minimal literature regarding the effectiveness of social media tools in an academic library context, there has been much written elsewhere, particularly in the marketing sector, which highlights the importance of monitoring 'fans', 'likes', 'followers' and 'comments'. It should be noted, however, that many authors (McClary, 2012; Walter, 2010; Marr, 2012) are also questioning the use of these metrics in assessing impact, arguing that there is a need to look beyond these simple metrics in favour of analytics tools such as Facebook Insights.[3]

Facebook Insights is a powerful tool which can help track user interaction. Insights can be set up from within Facebook and offers a wealth of potential data and metrics which can provide information on how customers interact with Facebook pages. Functionality which supports decision-making includes:

- the ability to regularly track fan size growth and usage spikes
- using the average number of likes or comments to gauge engagement by identifying which discussions are of more interest
- the option to view 'unlikes' and attrition rates – correlating these with the activity on library pages may help explain why people are leaving
- demographic information, including gender, age and location, which may offer an insight into audience and reach.

Marr (2012) outlines a number of strategies for evaluating Facebook presence and supports the assertion that 'over-simplified metrics such as the number of likes on Facebook . . . and the number of followers on Twitter . . . are good starting points but will actually tell you very little'. He believes it is important to have a strategy in mind linked to clear metrics of success, measures of engagement, such as the conversion rate (in the library context this could be increased use of online scholarly resources). In addition, Marr suggests monitoring search engine ranking and traffic from social media platforms and increased influence using the Klout score.[4] Klout purports to measure an individual's influence across a range of social media such as Twitter, Facebook and Google by analysing data on the size of an individual's network, the content created and how it is interacted with.

Conversely, Narayan (2012, 1) describes the difficulty in obtaining any meaningful measurement of the return on investment with regard to social media, attributing this to the burden of numbers (likes, follows, comments, views, shares) and the impossibility in most scenarios of isolating cause. He asserts, however, that the popularity of social media induces a naïve 'hope that the ever-evasive ROI formula will finally be revealed in a flash of blinding light, paving the way for continued investments into social media'.

Time for retirement

The literature also provides evidence that some digital reference technologies have been retired. In a survey undertaken by Chu and Du it was reported that

> Some tools had been, or would be, abandoned in the future. One library had used Second Life for some time, but it was too time-consuming to be continued . . . It was also reported a library blog was stopped because students did not like using it . . . Another library intended to stop using Facebook and Twitter because student interest in them was low . . . In this current study, libraries who planned

to adopt or abandon certain social networking tools indicated that they assessed the tools based on their beliefs and experiences . . . time requirements and operating costs.   Chu and Du, 2013, 8

This suggests that virtual reference technologies are subject to an adoption lifecycle based largely on volume of student use. Some technologies have a long lifespan, for example, e-mail, whereas others are short; identifying and adopting new means of connecting and interacting with users and abandoning tools that fail to deliver is therefore to be expected.

Evolution not revolution

What is clear from the literature describing the history of virtual reference is that it has been a process of evolution and not a revolution. Reference 2.0 utilizes new and different tools with which to connect with users but it must still be considered a refinement of the reference services that libraries have long provided (Partridge et al., 2010). Nevertheless, discussions of Library 2.0 and Reference 2.0 have also included an acknowledgement that the social web has changed the way libraries and librarians connect with users. There is also consensus that a new type of LIS professional, dubbed 'Librarian 2.0', is required, who can meet and connect with users in their online spaces (Abraham, 2005; Partridge et al., 2010) and have the ability to work in what Stephens (2006, 8) describes as a state of 'permanent beta'.

This chapter now turns to a case study of an Australian university in order to illustrate an approach to developing a virtual reference service.

Case study: the University of Western Australia

The University of Western Australia (UWA) is a medium-size institution with a current enrolment of 25,000 students and is a member of the Group of Eight Australian research-intensive universities. Information Services (IS) provides integrated information technology and library services to staff and students at the University. The section within IS responsible for the provision of reference services is Research and Learning Support, which comprises six subject libraries loosely aligned with the UWA faculty structure.

The history of reference services at UWA largely mirrors that described in the literature review. Face-to-face and telephone reference services were supplemented with e-mail reference services in the late 1990s and eventually evolved into the Ask a Librarian e-mail service in the early 2000s. This service provided an online form in which users could enter queries, selecting the relevant subject library from a drop-down list. Librarians would then respond to users directly via e-mail. In 2007, a project entitled 'Re-framing Information Services' investigated a variety of ways of enhancing reference services with technologies. The outcomes included an online suggestions blog, introduction of a chat reference service and adoption of askUWA, the University's enquiry management system.

askUWA[5]

UWA adopted the RightNow Enquiry Management System (branded askUWA) in 2007. Initially it was implemented within Student Services and the University was keen to see it become a central place for student-related frequently asked questions (FAQs) and enquiries. The library began using the service in 2008. Staff debated whether the e-mail Ask a Librarian service should continue to operate in parallel; however, it was decided that the use of one system would be more efficient and effective and the Ask a Librarian service was retired. All other enquiry-related e-mail addresses (each subject library had its own e-mail address for general enquiries) were directed to the askUWA system.

Implementation of askUWA required a complete re-think of the staffing model for virtual reference. Enquiries submitted via the previous Ask a Librarian service had been directed to subject library staff, whereas askUWA adopted a tiered system where enquiries would be assessed and then either answered or referred onwards. This centralized method of dealing with enquiries required a different way of working; a group of senior library officers were rostered to respond to or refer on tier 1 enquiries, with tier 2 groups created for librarians within each subject library, as well as for other specialist services such as document delivery.

In 2013 Research and Learning Support began to offer student IT support and a number of FAQs for student IT support were added to askUWA. The addition of student IT support has significantly increased the number of FAQ views and enquiries, with 3724 FAQ views and 207 enquiries submitted in the month of February 2013.

From the user's perspective the implementation of askUWA has resulted in a central place for student help. The system is set up so that users are presented with FAQs first and submit an enquiry only if they are unable to find an answer to their question. Users can also view all the questions and responses that they have submitted for easy referral. Benefits to the library include the ability to obtain statistics on response times, identify themes, create new FAQs and review the responses provided. The system tracks all enquiries and responses, provides standardization of greetings and salutations and provides good statistical detail.

Online suggestions blog

Blog functionality was identified as suitable for a suggestions scheme, as it enables users to send suggestions, and for the library to view and respond to suggestions. The suggestions blog[6], established in 2010, also allows responses to be submitted anonymously. The staffing model for the blog is the same as for askUWA.

Chat

A real-time chat reference service was introduced in 2010; however, a decision was made early in 2012 to retire the system due to its low use.

Facebook and Twitter

The IS Facebook and Twitter presence have grown organically since they were created in 2009. While they are mainly used for promotion, news and notifications, IS recognize the potential for traditional reference services to be delivered via this medium. To address this, IS is developing a strategy which will draw upon the framework for development and evaluation outlined later in this chapter.

A snapshot of Virtual Reference 2.0 in Australian academic libraries

In the process of conducting the literature review it became apparent that there was no clear picture of the virtual reference landscape in Australian academic libraries. To this end, the authors undertook a survey of current practice across the sector to bridge this gap and to inform the development of an IS strategy for social media at UWA.

Methodology

The survey aimed to gather feedback from Australian academic libraries to determine:

- the tools and technologies being used to provide virtual reference services
- use of, satisfaction with and effectiveness of the tools and technologies
- evaluation of the tools and technologies used
- adoption of strategy and policy
- staff development
- tools and technologies no longer in use.

An online survey using the software programme Qualtrics was sent out via e-mail to all 39 Australian academic libraries. It was completed by 20 libraries, giving a response rate of 51% with at least one response received from each Australian State and Territory.

Reference 2.0: the snapshot findings
Policies

To the question whether there was a policy on the use of the systems either within the library or the broader university, the overwhelming response was yes, with all respondents having a policy on Facebook and Twitter and all but two having a policy on e-mail. In contrast, replies about a policy on the evaluation of the systems gave a more mixed picture. The majority of responses said there was a policy of evaluation for university enquiry management systems but for chat, wikis, instant messaging, Facebook and Twitter there were an equal number of answers that said yes or no. As stated previously all respondents had a policy for Facebook and Twitter; however, only seven (35%) responded that they had a policy on their evaluation. For e-mail reference services there were more responses that stated they did not have a policy on evaluation than did. There was a tendency to cover the evaluation of a number of systems through a social media policy either already in place or soon to be implemented.

Communication tools

E-mail, the original platform for virtual reference, remains the most common tool of choice for providing virtual reference services, as it was used by all of the university libraries who responded. The social media tools Facebook and Twitter were being used by all but two academic libraries surveyed (98%). The survey also revealed that while some real-time technologies such as chat and instant messaging are not as popular, the libraries that use them are satisfied with their use. Figure 2.1 shows the tools and systems most widely used across the Australian academic library sector.

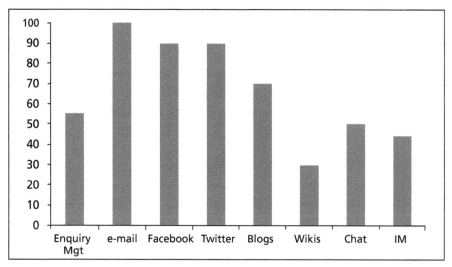

Figure 2.1   *Virtual reference tools and systems most used in Australian academic libraries*

Other systems used for communication with staff and students included FAQs, Yammer (a private communication tool), LibGuides and learning management systems such as Moodle, as well as other online tools (Blackboard Collaborate, Skype, YouTube, Flickr and Instagram).

Respondents were asked to describe the purpose of the technologies in use. Based on the responses, e-mail and Facebook were utilized for a variety of purposes (enquiries, feedback, notices, promotion and news). Twitter was described as useful for promotion and 'checking sentiments expressed about [the library] and social conversation'. There was much similarity in how libraries described their use of blogs (promotion, internal communication, news, suggestion and feedback), chat (responding to queries in real time) and wikis (staff collaboration, internal knowledge sharing).

Perhaps not surprisingly, the functions of each technology largely determined how they were applied in practice, for example, chat was used for real-time quick enquiry submission and response, whereas e-mail was used for both first-tier and longer enquiries, as well as for sharing information about resources and activities.

Twitter and Facebook enabled libraries to adopt a more informal approach and they were often used interchangeably. In addition Facebook was widely used as a means of encouraging social interaction, relationship building and student engagement and this was distinctly different to the way other systems were reported as being used. There was, however, some evidence that the different social media systems were used in a joined-up way, for example, Twitter was used to promote blog posts and Facebook status updates.

University enquiry management systems are used as expected, for a range of front-end (submitting and responding) and back-end (forwarding and tracking) queries as well as compiling a database of FAQs for access 24/7.

Emergence of virtual reference one-stop shops

While the survey results clearly indicate that various technologies are being employed for the purpose of digital reference, with libraries tending to create a number of different virtual service points, some respondents described the successful use of university-based enquiry systems as opposed to those which were library-based. In a number of instances the RightNow system had been adopted for the entire university, with the library using it as their primary online enquiry system. Respondents described the potential of one-stop shops to simplify the experience of users who care little about organizational structures by creating the virtual online one-stop shop, with the option to access FAQs or submit queries on a range of topics to multiple parts of the university.

One academic library reported that it had recently adopted the Springshare product LibAnswers,[7] which was 'useful in tying together previously separate online services (chat, e-mail and Q&As) as well as improving statistics keeping' in a move towards an integrated virtual reference service.

A few respondents also utilized their university's Twitter or Facebook pages. Although this is contrary to the majority of survey responses, it does suggest an alternative model worth exploring, since university accounts usually have more fans and followers. This route seemingly has the potential for the library to engage more effectively with its widest audience.

Measuring performance and return on investment

When asked how satisfied they were with the systems they used, 14 respondents (70%) indicated that they were satisfied or very satisfied with Twitter and 15 (80%) with e-mail. Most responses were neutral, satisfied or very satisfied, indicating that academic libraries are comfortable with the tools they are using.

It is interesting to note, however, that the number of daily queries or posts submitted to the various systems was universally low, although the volume of queries submitted to each system varied from library to library, with Facebook and Twitter having the fewest number per day from the majority of respondents. Fourteen respondents (75%) had less than two queries per day on Facebook, while sixteen (85%) had less than two on Twitter.

E-mail meanwhile received more queries for the majority of respondents. This was between two and ten queries per day with two respondents receiving ten to twenty queries a day (during semester time).

Two of the ten libraries using chat said they received one to two queries per day and no one reported that they received more than ten queries per day. Five of the respondents (25%) said they had retired chat within their academic library on the grounds of low usage or lack of demand compared to the staff time required to run the service.

While one might consider one to two chat queries per day quite low given the staffing resource required to monitor a real-time service, respondents using chat were most satisfied with its use compared with the other systems, giving it the highest mean score of 4.60 out of 5. University enquiry management systems were rated next at 4.33, followed by e-mail at 4.17. Facebook and Twitter were rated slightly lower at 3.78 and 3.89 respectively. Therefore, despite their popularity, it is believed they can be improved upon.

The majority of respondents reported that they measured the effectiveness of the systems they used. Of the nineteen respondents who used Facebook, fourteen said they measured its effectiveness (70%). Measures of effectiveness included Google Analytics, page likes, statistics, chat transcription and the general scrutiny by library management. Almost two-thirds (65%) of the respondents measured the effectiveness of e-mail. Measures of effectiveness included statistics (e-mails received and response times), response quality analysis and feedback from users.

Structured methods were used to gather feedback, such as user surveys developed both in-house and externally using Insync Surveys (an Australian provider of academic library surveys), alongside focus groups, online forms and ad hoc comments received through the systems themselves or suggestion schemes. Blogs were less likely to be evaluated by respondents. Wikis were not evaluated at all by those who responded and we hypothesize that this is likely to be because in the libraries in our survey they are used almost exclusively for internal information sharing.

Librarian 2.0 – staff training and development

Staff supporting the various systems were considered as key to the success of initiatives. When asked if libraries actively develop staff expertise in these systems, responses varied depending on the systems used, with the majority stating that university enquiry management systems, chat, Facebook and Twitter were the areas where staff expertise was most actively developed. The top two systems where staff development was considered necessary were Twitter, with 13 responses (65%) and Facebook, with 11 responses (55%). Training was the main method used across the board, with guidelines also provided, along with mentoring and coaching. Staff receiving training varied between individuals who expressed an interest, groups defined by job role, or in some cases all staff.

Retiring systems

The system most likely to be retired was blogs (30% of respondents) with chat (25%) and wikis (21%) following closely. None of the respondents had retired Facebook or Twitter. To the question why the systems had been retired a variety of responses were received, e.g. the system was difficult to use, it failed to meet the stated needs or was superseded by another system. Overwhelmingly the main reason given was low usage by clients and in some cases this was linked to the amount of staff effort required which was considered disproportionate to the benefit derived.

Success factors and a framework for development and evaluation

In rating the factors that make virtual reference initiatives successful, the highest ranked response was policy and strategy, with eight responses (40%) ranking it as the most important. This was followed by effective staff support with five responses (25%) and then staff enthusiasm and engagement with four (20%). Promotion and marketing was ranked next, followed by evaluation and feedback.

The continuous review and improvement of systems was ranked very low as a success factor by the majority of participants. Knowledge of the client base and their communication preferences was considered important by a few as was providing engaging and interesting content to attract and retain users. Student engagement and long-term library and staff commitment were also mentioned, as was access to a broad range of communication channels.

A framework for Reference 2.0

Based on the authors' professional experience, the literature review and survey findings, we are tentatively offering a framework to inform the selection, development and evaluation of an effective Reference 2.0 service. The elements of the framework set out in Table 2.1 have been identified as critical success factors in the development and evaluation of digital enquiry services.

Table 2.1 *A framework for developing and evaluating digital enquiry services* Source: Dawn McLoughlin and Jill Benn, University of Western Australia	
Strategy and policy	A strategy and policy regarding the use and evaluation of tools, describing how they relate to one another and how they are linked to the priorities of the wider organization.
Goals	Well defined, measurable goals (or objectives) aligned with the priorities of the wider organization, which are regularly reviewed against performance.
Workforce development	Provide training and development for staff delivering the services. Encourage staff experimentation with new technologies. Develop skills in creating engaging content. Sell the benefits to win hearts and minds.
Audience(s)	Develop an in-depth understanding of the defined audience(s). Use system data to find out who your virtual reference users are. Look beyond the library pages. Find out where your users go online. Investigate how clients discover, navigate and interpret the virtual reference systems on offer.
Marketing and Promotion	Develop a marketing and promotion strategy which outlines customer segments and preferences which are linked to promotional activities.
Evaluation and Review	Develop an evaluation plan which outlines the process for determining whether digital reference tools are providing value. Identify specialist tools for evaluation, for example Facebook Insights or Google Analytics. Be prepared to retire tools not meeting desired goals. Actively include users in the evaluation process.
Horizon scanning	Keep abreast of new technologies and their application and benchmark with other services.

Conclusion

Digital enquiry services are now firmly embedded within Australian academic libraries, with social media tools such as Facebook and Twitter working alongside more traditional virtual reference tools such as e-mail and chat. The process of change has been evolutionary rather than revolutionary but it is clear that the social web has changed the way libraries and librarians now connect with their users. What is less clear, however, is the impact or value Reference 2.0 is delivering: over-reliance on simple metrics such as 'likes' or followers reveals little about how users' attitudes or behaviour may have been influenced. The survey showed that there is relatively low use of some systems and that meaningful evaluation methods are yet to be determined, although analytics tools such as Facebook Insights and Klout show great promise.

We observed that some academic libraries are converging their reference services and embracing the concept of a virtual 'one-stop shop'. By aligning virtual reference services with core priorities and by employing a framework for development and evaluation (including policy and strategy) it is possible, we believe, to deliver service offering increased value and impact. Our survey suggests that there may also be benefits to libraries and users in adopting a more centralized approach.

Further research opportunities include the correlation between physical and virtual service points in providing a seamless user experience and integration, appraising methods of measuring virtual reference effectiveness and, finally, understanding the impact of Reference 2.0 on staffing models, roles and skills.

Notes

1   www.timeshighereducation.co.uk/world-university-rankings/2013/reputation-ranking.
2   www.arwu.org/.
3   www.facebook.com/insights.
4   www.klout.com/corp/klout_score.
5   www.uwa.edu.au/askuwa.
6   http://suggestions.is.uwa.edu.au.
7   http://springshare.com/libanswers.

References

Abraham, S. (2005) Web 2.0—Huh?! Library 2.0, Librarian 2.0, *Information Outlook*, www.scribd.com/doc/247521/InfoTech-Dec2005.
Aguilar, K., Keating, K., Schadl, S. and Van Reenen, J. (2011) Reference as Outreach:

meeting users where they are, *Journal of Library Administration*, **51**, 343–58.

American Library Association (2004) Guidelines for Implementing and Maintaining Virtual Reference Services, MARS Digital Reference Guidelines Ad Hoc Committee, Reference and User Services Association, www.ala.org/rusa/resources/guidelines/virtrefguidelines.

Arya, H. B. and Mishra, J. K. (2011) Oh! Web 2.0, Virtual Reference Service 2.0, Tools & Techniques (1): a basic approach, *Journal of Library and Information Services in Distance Learning*, **5** (4), 149–71.

Chad, K. and Miller, P. (2005) *Do Libraries Matter? The rise of Library 2.0*, http://jclspscwiki.jocolibrary.org/images/4/42/Background_Reading_-_Do_ Libraries_Matter.pdf.

Charnigo, L. and Barnett-Ellis, P. (2007) Checking out Facebook.com: the impact of a digital trend on academic libraries, *Information Technology and Libraries*, **26** (1), 23–34, www.ala.org/lita/ital/sites/ala.org.lita.ital/files/content/26/1/charnigo.pdf.

Chu, S. K. W. and Du, H. (2013) Social Networking Tools for Academic Libraries, *Journal of Librarianship & Information Science*, **45** (1), 64–75.

Conyers, A. and Payne, P. (2011) Library Performance Measurement in the Digital Age. In Dale, J. and Holland M. (eds), *University Libraries and Digital Learning Environments*, Ashgate, http://eprints.bbk.ac.uk/2958.

De Rosa, C., Cantrell J., Havens, A., Hawk, J. and Jenkins, L. (2007) *Sharing, Privacy and Trust in Our Networked World: a report to the OCLC membership*, OCLC, www.oclc.org/reports/pdfs/sharing.pdf.

Fritch, J. and Mandernack, S. (2001) The Emerging Reference Paradigm: a vision of reference services in a complex information environment, *Library Trends*, **50** (2), 286–305.

Glazer, H. (2012) 'Likes' are Lovely, but Do They Lead to More Logins? Developing metrics for academic libraries' Facebook pages, *College & Research Libraries News*, **73** (1), 18–21, http://crln.acrl.org/content/73/1/18.full.

Hosny, M. and Fatima, S. (2012) Facebook in Education: students, teachers and library perspectives, *Journal of Computing*, **4** (6), www.scribd.com/doc/100492727/Facebook-in-Education-Students-Teachers-and-Library-Perspectives.

Jackson, R. (2002) Revolution or Evolution: reference planning in ARL libraries, *Reference Services Review*, **20** (3), 212–28.

Janes, J. (2008) An Informal History (and Possible Future) of Digital Reference, *Bulletin of the American Society for Information Science and Technology*, **34** (2), 8–10, www.asis.org/Bulletin/Dec-07/DecJan08_Janes.pdf.

Levinson, R. (1988) New I & R Teams in Library-Based Services: librarians, social workers and older volunteers. In Katz, W. and Middleton, M. (eds), *Information and Referral in Reference Services*, Haworth Press, New York.

Marr, B. (2012) *Measuring your Facebook ROI!*, www.linkedin.com/today/post/ article/20121114155039-64875646-measuring-your-facebook-roi.

McClary, T. (2012) *How to Measure Your Success on Facebook*, http://marketing.njstatelib.org/blog/2012/oct/19/tmcclary/how_to_measure_your_ success_on_facebook.

Narayan, L. (2012) 3 Reasons Why There's No Measuring ROI on Social Media, *Forbes*, www.forbes.com/sites/ciocentral/2012/08/28/3-reasons-why-theres-no-measuring-roi-on-social-media/2.

Partridge, H., Menzies, V., Lee, J. and Munro, C. (2010) The Contemporary Librarian: skills, knowledge and attributes required in a world of emerging technologies, *Library & Information Science Research*, **32** (4), 265–71.

Sidorko, P. and Cmor, D. (2012) Does Generation Google REALLY Need Us?, paper presented at the World Library and Information Congress, 78th IFLA General Conference and Assembly, Helsinki, http://conference.ifla.org/past/ifla/78/98-sidorko-en.pdf.

Stephens, M. (2006) Into a New World of Librarianship: next space, *OCLC Newsletter 2*, www.oclc.org/nextspace/002/3.htm.

Stevens, C. (2013) Reference Reviewed and Re-Envisioned: revamping librarian and desk-centric Services with LibStARs and LibAnswers, *Journal of Academic Librarianship*, **39** (2), www.sciencedirect.com/science/article/pii/S0099133312001747.

Walter, E. (2010) *A Beginner's Guide to Facebook Insights*, http://mashable.com/2010/09/03/facebook-insights-guide.

CHAPTER 3

A service in transition: how digital technology is shaping organizational change

Rachel Bury and Helen Jamieson

Introduction

As devices and connectivity become increasingly affordable and portable they have transformed how we do business, learn, organize our leisure time and manage our relationships. Inevitably, these technological innovations have been long-term drivers of change within academic libraries. It is now for example, nearly two decades since the emergence of the 'hybrid library': a physical library, performing traditional roles but also delivering services in digital as well as print format. Digital technologies have also enabled libraries to transform their operations and make considerable efficiency savings while continuing to expand their services. Yet there is a real risk that much of what academic libraries do is invisible to users in a virtual environment, resulting in 'a strong feeling among senior librarians that they have failed effectively to communicate the value of their services to those who fund and use them' (RIN and SCONUL, 2010, 16).

Past practices at marketing library services are seemingly no longer meeting the needs of users who increasingly live in a digital world. The emergence of the social web, characterized by user-generated connections, conversations and content, is causing many libraries to rethink how they develop and manage their relationships with users. As a consequence, many academic library services are now being reconfigured with resources (staff and content) being moved to where there is greatest impact – to those services that support the learning lives and workflows of their users.

This chapter describes how one UK academic library has through strategy and service planning sought to refocus attention on the user. In a critical appraisal of the distance travelled, it will discuss the importance of understanding library users' behaviour and workflows, the role of strategic marketing, how the use of digital and social media supports the library 'brand' and how all staff have a role to play in terms of advocacy and relationship management.

Framing the discussion
Strategy and focus

In a world increasingly shaped by digital technologies and, at this time in the UK, by austerity, fresh thinking is needed to understand what a library now means and what it does to ensure that its strategic focus is on resourcing those areas that will have the biggest impact on users (RIN and SCONUL, 2010). This view is reinforced by Dempsey, who argues that libraries

> cannot continue to spend a lot of time on activities that are being done elsewhere and do not create real value for their institutions. Strategy is about making choices that increase impact. It is about moving resources to where there is most benefit, and finding the right level at which things should be done.
>
> Dempsey, 2012, 121

What does 'moving resources' mean in practice? RIN and SCONUL (2010) argue that libraries across the UK HE sector have already achieved significant efficiency savings through using technology to lower the costs of transactions or interactions, for example through implementing self-issue. The strategic focus has moved from library transactions and even collections to ensuring that libraries can continue to position themselves as key partners within their institution by sourcing new infrastructure to meet changing user needs because

> the library is now a part only of the information universe. Many of its approaches were developed to manage when resources were scarce. . . . Previously researchers/learners would build their workflow around the library. Now the library must build its services around the user workflow. The library has to think about how to get into those flows.
>
> Dempsey, 2012, 123

This view is reinforced by the recent publication of a major survey of UK academics, which has revealed an increasing reliance on the internet as a starting point for research or resources. Of the survey's 3498 participants,

40% said that when beginning a project they start by searching the internet for relevant materials, with only 2% visiting the physical library as a first port of call. Furthermore, if researchers could not find the resources or information they needed through their university library, 90% would look online for a freely available version (Housewright, Schonfield and Wulfson, 2013).

If the library must now rethink its services in order to wrap around and engage with the user workflow then it must stop trying to persuade users to change their behaviour to fit the library 'offer' and instead develop a deeper understanding of the workflows and learning lives of its users. In other words, libraries must stop 'selling' their collections and services and adopt a customer-centred marketing approach.

Changing mind-sets: from library-centred to customer-centred

Marketing, according to Kotler and Andreasen (1991, 43) starts 'with customer perceptions, needs and wants'. They go on to state that if a customer-centred approach to marketing is to be successful, then it should be understood and 'owned' by senior managers. Within a library context, therefore, the two prerequisites of a customer-centred, strategic approach to marketing must be a top-down commitment to this approach and the will to divert time and resources to the creation of a marketing culture at all levels of the library. This is further discussed in more recent literature revealing a shift from a piecemeal approach to the 'selling' of products and services towards a strategic, customer-centred approach (Nunn and Rouane, 2011; Gall, 2010; Estall and Stephens, 2011).

Customer satisfaction, according to Mathews (2009), is an important predictor of a customer's future behaviour and whether they are likely to recommend to others. He also argues that the role of advocates and partnerships in building relationships with customers are of central importance. This is reinforced by Gupta (2002), who asserts that marketing your library service cannot be seen as something separate from individual staff roles; all staff must embrace and embed a marketing approach within their daily work.

Adoption of a successful customer-centred marketing approach can, however, be challenging. Estall and Stephens (2011) and Singh (2009) found that library staff often have a weak understanding of what marketing means, frequently equating it with 'selling' and negative connotations of hype and poor ethics. These authors argue that decision-making is less likely to be based on users' identified needs and more likely to be based on staff expertise and intuition. They point out that staff cannot be expected to have the knowledge and skills necessary to operationalize a marketing strategy if they do not know what it means in the context of their organization.

Social networks, user workflows and learning lives

While academic library users now have access to a distributed web of print and online information within and beyond the library, it is more likely to be through their networks of people connected through social media that they will, according to Hagel III, Seely Brown and Davison (2012), gain effective entry points to information curated by practitioners or pundits and considered by the user to be credible or trustworthy. Dempsey (2012, 125), concurring with this view, asserts that libraries and librarians should understand that 'it is increasingly important to understand the dynamics of social and research networks, and about writing/communicating on the web'.

Hagel III, Seely Brown and Davison (2010) frame their thinking about how people and organizations should position themselves to operate effectively in a digital and networked society by identifying three consecutive levels of performance: *access*, *attract* and *achieve*. The first level, *access*, is the ability to find people and resources when needed. *Attract* is the ability to connect with people who are important in some respect to you and *achieve* is the ability to engage or collaborate with those people and translate that into improved performance. Dempsey, in applying this framework in relation to academic libraries, makes two important observations; first, if libraries and librarians want to be regarded as 'expert' then their expertise should be seen, and second, that within the next ten years the successful positioning of libraries will to a large extent depend upon participation in 'networks of people and resources facilitated by digital networks' (Dempsey, 2012, 120).

From an academic library perspective, the authors have identified a missing level, which is *assess*; the extent to which libraries understand their users' perceptions, needs and experience and also the means through which performance in these new areas of digital networking is measured.

One academic library in transition

The following case study aims to draw together the themes discussed in the previous sections, by using the experience of one university library undertaking a strategic approach to becoming a customer-centred service. Using the Hagel III, Seely Brown and Davison (2010) framework of Access, Attract and Achieve (with the inclusion of Assess), it will describe some of the service initiatives that exemplify its strategic marketing approach and conclude with a critical appraisal of their impact to date.

Context

Edge Hill University is a campus-based university based in the north-west of England. The University has a student population of over 22,000 and 1300 staff. This includes a full-time student population of around 10,100 and the UK's largest number of postgraduates, many studying on advanced professional development programmes. It is one of the fastest-growing universities in the country, with a fourfold increase in applications in the last decade.

Learning Services (also referred to as 'the Service') is one of the largest support departments within the University, with approximately 130 staff based across four main libraries as well as a number of outreach centres. Learning Services includes library, support for academic skills, information and communications technology (ICT) and specific learning difficulties (SpLD), media development and technology enhanced learning.

Within the Service, marketing had historically been carried out on an ad hoc basis without an underlying strategy or formalized plan. Responsibility for marketing or marketing activities was not part of a defined role and was largely associated with specific promotional events 'selling' services and collections using face-to-face interaction (Bury and Phillips, 2008). A commitment to a strategic approach to marketing that would raise the Service's visibility began with the introduction of two important new posts: Quality, Communication and Marketing Manager and specialist web and graphic designer. Initial work focused on unravelling assumptions about marketing and gaining a better understanding of, and rebuilding relationships with, different user groups. As Alcock (2011, 38) explains, 'relationship marketing [is] focusing on more long term marketing efforts to discover customers' needs and preferences, and using this information to build a relationship with customers (and potential customers)'.

Taking heed of these key messages, a number of briefings and activities and staff development were introduced to provide all staff with a greater awareness of marketing, the role of the Quality, Communication and Marketing Manager and more importantly their contribution to the marketing plan. A short value proposition or value statement was developed to encapsulate the core beliefs that underpin the Service ethos:

- Customer Excellence: our product is high-quality support and resources
- Operational Excellence: our operational systems and processes are customer-focused and effective
- Staff Engagement: our staff drive our customer and operational excellence improvements.

The purpose of the value statement is to help create connections with Service users. It is also used to support staff understanding of the core Service principles or values in order to help focus direction for the Service. The focus then turned to identifying priority areas for attention and Alcock's (2011) survey questions were used to gather feedback from staff on their perception of marketing, its importance and value to the Service as a strategic activity. The outcome from this feedback-gathering exercise has resulted in a number of initiatives:

- the development of a strategic marketing plan agreed at a senior level and shared across the whole Service
- internal promotion by the Quality, Communication and Marketing Manager
- an annual activity planner, introduced to help co-ordinate all marketing related activities and improve staff awareness and engagement
- staff development opportunities targeted at groups of staff to enable them to explore key concepts of marketing and use of social media in libraries
- regular opportunities for staff to discuss and review user feedback.

Access: being visible and seen as credible

If *access*, as defined by Hagel III, Seely Brown and Davison (2010), is the ability to find people and resources when needed, then the web has a key role in signposting library expertise and resources to its users. In considering *access* from an academic library perspective, Dempsey (2012) asks librarians to consider whether library expertise and resources are readily visible when people are searching their website and whether library users can easily discover personal contacts or staff photographs on their website.

A new approach to displaying Learning Services' web content and bringing staff expertise and resources to the fore was a considered to be a priority. The web pages were dated and in need of an overhaul. Access management was also an important issue, as the pages had been constructed using what had become a legacy product. With the availability of new software to manage design, content, news and editorial rights, a radical change was possible.

Usability testing of the proposed website was an important first step to ensure that the approach to content, layout and structure would meet users' needs. The results were used to inform decisions about language, style and content hierarchy. Usability testing and consultation with both non-users and users was undertaken in collaboration with colleagues in the central IT Services web services team. This collaborative approach was crucial both in terms of the changes and improvements to the web pages and access to tools to improve communication with users. These web design specialists proved to be a valuable source of expertise in helping Learning Services to make informed choices with regard to its digital presence and service promotion.

The new website[1] has sought to bring library expertise and resources to the fore. Figure 3.1 on the following page illustrates how the redesign has introduced a regularly updated 'librarian recommends' section with a photograph and contact information featuring prominently on the introductory page of each subject resources section.

Assess: bringing the learning lives of library users into sharper focus

To ensure that services are wrapped around customer needs and not librarians' perceptions of their needs, Learning Services employs a wide range of techniques to 'get to know' its customers, to understand how different customers prefer to be consulted and how they prefer to engage with the Service.

Customer segmentation

Undertaking a customer segmentation process to identify subsets of library users who have common needs has been particularly helpful in designing and targeting services to meet those needs. Staff at all levels of Learning Services are involved in the segmentation process and, as a living document, the segmentation document is revisited annually to ensure that it remains current.

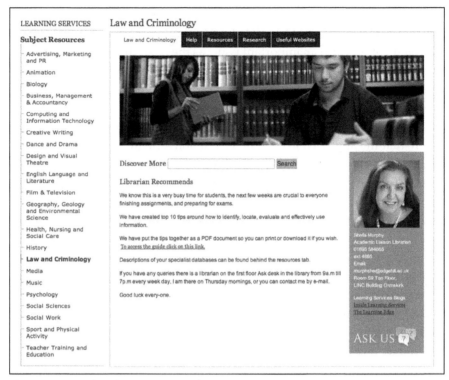

Figure 3.1   *'Librarian recommends'*
Source: EHU (reproduced with permission)

Obtaining qualitative and quantitative data

In common with libraries everywhere, Learning Services uses both qualitative and quantitative information and data ranging from activity data[2] generated from user interactions, whether online or physical (for example, book loans, downloads), to surveys and focus groups. Other more innovative mechanisms the Service has adopted include participant and non-participant observations and customer journey mapping,[3] which describes all the experiences a customer has with an organization and the positive and negative emotional responses they provoke.

Non-participation observation, an ethnographic technique, has been found to be particularly useful, with staff occupying learning spaces alongside students and recording the tasks, activities and more importantly, the behaviours they observe. Using multiple data generation methods allows Learning Services to cross-verify the credibility of data that purports to provide a better understanding of how students are using its services, how satisfied they are with them and whether services, resources and facilities are meeting their needs.

Understanding how students use technology

As well as more general data about library use and satisfaction, Learning Services has started to better understand how students interact with the Service using technology. National and international data shows that growth in mobile device ownership is increasing exponentially. The research undertaken by Google and Ipsos (2012) provides evidence that mobile device ownership is now mainstream, with the UK showing the largest increase in smartphone ownership in the previous 12 months, from 30% to 45% of the total population. In considering how students are using technology, Calder, Thaney and Killingworth's (2013) research found that 67% of students use technology at least once an hour. Although these are interesting figures and a useful broad brush for understanding user behaviour around technology, Learning Services was mindful of the need to find out what was happening locally.

Learning Services has actively been growing its evidence base around student use of technology. It now has five years' worth of longitudinal data available from its student e-Learning survey. This annual 'snapshot' was initiated by a desire to improve the student experience through a better understanding of what made for a good experience of technology-enhanced learning. It also provides an indicator of the extent to which the institutional virtual learning environment (VLE) is integral to the learning experience of Edge Hill students. The survey questions are intended to identify student experiences and expectations and include use of electronic resources, preferred place(s) of study, student ownership of technology and the frequency of its use and use of social media (Martin, 2012). A much richer picture is obtained when the survey data is triangulated with activity data from the VLE, Google Analytics, the library management system and other transactional data (for example, the volume and nature of enquiries at help desks).

With regard to the use of mobile technologies, the survey, which is reinforced by VLE and website activity data, suggests that personal access to mobile devices is now mainstream within the Edge Hill University student population, with 65% of students saying that they regularly use their smartphone in the University's Wi-Fi spaces. Figure 3.2 (on the next page) shows the trends in student ownership of mobile devices since 2008/9.

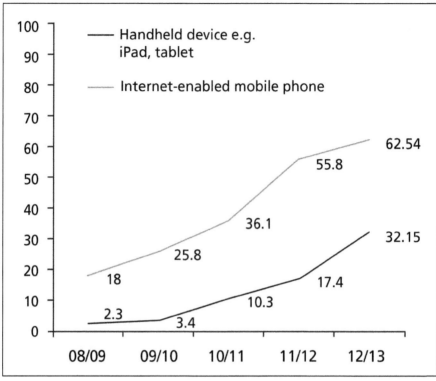

Figure 3.2   *Edge Hill student mobile device ownership since 2008/9*
Source: EHU (reproduced with permission)

Yet students still expect the University to provide open-access computers for their use and 67% of survey respondents claim to make regular use of them. However, 54.2% of students also regularly use their own laptops on campus. A continuing upward trend of smartphone and tablet ownership shows 60.4% of respondents accessing the VLE via a mobile device and 64.9% regularly using their smartphones in Edge Hill's Wi-Fi-enabled spaces. It is interesting to note that although Wi-Fi is available across the campus, students still prefer to study in library-supported areas, which suggests that although access to resources is now more mobile, the library continues to play a key role on as well as off campus. However, the data on Edge Hill students' mobile device ownership and use has challenged the Service's long-standing notion of students seeking help-desk support for technical issues arising from their use of computers. The snapshot provided by the survey, reinforced by data from other sources, has prompted a reappraisal of how Learning Services can best support students using mobile devices and what corresponding knowledge and skills are needed by staff.

Case study: mobile and marketing

The rapidly increasing use of mobile devices by students for accessing information and communication described in the previous section has prompted a reappraisal of how Learning Services can best support students who use mobile devices. In order that students can use their mobile devices to the full it is necessary for library staff to keep pace with or increase their skills in relation to mobile technology so that they become comfortable and familiar with the hardware and software. To this end, Learning Services introduced a 'buddy', co-mentoring approach: subject librarians paired with learning technologists to encourage sharing of expertise. It was a reciprocal exercise, with librarians learning more about technology and technologists learning more about subject-related resources and services. Android tablets or iPads, depending on preferences, were purchased for subject librarians to enable them to become familiar with the technology and for use in supporting students or when working with academics away from the office.

The Service has also introduced mobile technology clinics where staff and students can bring along their mobile devices and talk to staff about getting connected with Wi-Fi, best practice, choosing and downloading apps, and accessing resources. These clinics are held outside the library in high-traffic areas across campus such as the student hub which houses the student union, catering outlets and open access to computers. As well as serving the practical purpose of supporting the use of mobile devices and offering troubleshooting advice at these clinics, Learning Services staff have used these activities to raise their visibility and present themselves to all stakeholders as approachable technology and resources 'experts'. The clinics also give staff the opportunity to engage with users, to ask them questions about what they use their devices for and what they perceive to be the barriers to accessing library resources, the VLE and appropriate support.

Learning Services has also taken the decision to employ students to offer roving peer-to-peer support within the University library. These student assistants are provided with iPads so that they can support students at their point of need, for example, in the book stock or at a computer. From 2013 the student assistants have also 'roved' beyond the library into other spaces on campus where students gather when not in taught sessions. In addition to offering help and support, the assistants have conducted a survey to obtain student feedback on services and resources. Indeed, the assistants reported that having a task to complete made it easier to approach students and engage them in conversation. Having an online survey uploaded onto the assistants' iPads also ensured the student responses were automatically collated and could be analysed 'on the go'.

In the initial pilot for engaging with users outside the physical library building the student assistants roved the campus every day for a two-week period. During that time they talked to 300 students outside the library, dealing with students' individual concerns around a wide range of basic enquiries that included finding books and journals, demonstrating electronic resources, referencing, mobile apps, using Facebook and Twitter to keep up to date, navigating Learning Services web pages, using reprographics equipment and resolving ICT issues.

Attract: harnessing social media to bring the library to the user

While improving access to staff expertise and resources makes them easier for users to find, their value is limited if the encounters are brief and one-directional. Experience shows that reciprocal relationships are based on trust and continuity. Building relationships with library users that result in purposeful engagement has not proved to be a quick or simple task: it has required significant staff time and effort. Digital and social media have proved to be a useful means of attracting and engaging with users by showcasing what the library has to offer, making the library and librarians seem more 'human'. The campaign 'Be a star of the silent library' represented a conscious shift away from 'telling' users to observe silence in the library, towards the use of humour as a means of influencing user behaviour. Figure 3.3 shows a campaign image published on plasma screens around the University. Campaigns are co-ordinated by the Quality, Communication and Marketing Manager and supported by the specialist web and graphic designer, who has been crucial in producing creative, high-quality images and information graphics.

To encourage staff to develop a 'voice' and build relationships with their user groups, another 'buddy' system allows them to practice and receive feedback on writing, using a wide range of social media. The role of Quality, Communication and Marketing Manager has been crucial in providing support, generating clarity and buy-in to the house style, selecting the most appropriate communication tools and encouraging teams and individual managers to be involved in writing. As a result, a growing number of staff actively contribute to Learning Services blogs, Facebook and Twitter accounts and to news items on the web pages. This is work in progress and in 2013 the focus has been on a Service-wide review of the communication

Figure 3.3   *Image for University plasma screens*
Source: EHU (reproduced with permission)

strategy, staff visibility and how they develop and manage relationships with users in the digital medium.

Nevertheless, Learning Services has made use of social media for a number of high-profile campaigns as a means of engaging in a two-way conversation with staff and students from across the University rather than simply pushing out information. One of the most successful campaigns to date has been the EHU Loves Reading Campaign: an attempt to promote reading for pleasure as well as for academic study, to open up the collections and highlight the range of fiction material that was available within the library. Figure 3.4 on the next page shows the campaign strapline and book/heart image used. Students and staff were asked to describe the books they were currently reading and explain why they loved reading in entries on the Learning Services blog, Facebook page and Twitter. Excitingly, a one-direction campaign became a multi-way conversation when other staff and students contributed their own experiences or commented upon what was being posted.

These marketing campaigns are not random; they are planned at the beginning of the academic year in order to link to the student life cycle as much as possible. A calendar shared with all staff across the Service lists all the campaigns, events and activities keeps them informed and able to support the key messages. In addition to the structured campaigns, Facebook and Twitter provide more frequent and informal communications

Figure 3.4 *EHU Loves Reading logo*
Source: EHU (reproduced with permission)

with the intention of keeping users 'warm'; for example, the 'official' library Twitter account generally tweets Service information but on Fridays is currently tweeting under the hashtag #flashbackfriday, posting old photographs of the University and library in order to invite comments.

This activity would not, of course, be possible without staff participation. The shared calendar is discussed at team meetings and has proved a useful means of involving front- and back-of-house staff in the generation of new ideas and messages that they think will be useful to users. The idea that *all* staff should be marketing advocates is one that is increasingly important in the culture of the Service, but experience has shown that this only works with staff buy-in. Only an informed and engaged workforce can operate effectively within their roles, providing excellent customer service and also acting as an ambassador or advocate for Learning Services. Building upon the progress achieved to date, the Service has now developed an internal communications framework to identify potential campaigns and provide consistent, regular and robust communication to ensure all staff are engaged in key activities and developments within their own team, the wider Service and the University.

Achieve: engaging with users in their own spaces

Encouragingly, the Service has observed a big increase in readership of its two blogs. The Learning Service blog[4] is used to publicize Service-wide initiatives, projects and important news (although news items now have a home on the web pages), whereas the Learning Edge blog[5] focuses on the use of the VLE and other technologies to enhance teaching and learning practice in the University. The growing blog readership (based on the number of 'hits' and repeat visitors according to monthly analysis of Google Analytics) is considered to be a result of a range of factors, of which the most important are:

- staff getting better at writing for the web
- more contributions and from a wider variety of staff
- greater visibility due to RSS blog feeds on the staff and student portals

- better timing of blog posts to ensure they have maximum exposure on the portals
- not using the blogs for general information (the basic premise is that blog posts must be relevant and of interest to customers).

Achieving two-way, productive conversations with users in social media spaces is proving the hardest of the Hagel III levels to attain . . . but it is possible, as the EHU Loves Reading social media campaign has demonstrated. This and other campaigns, along with regular staff contributions to social media, indicate that the Service is at least following the right direction of travel. As staff become more proficient in using social media, mobile technology and in writing in an engaging 'voice', it is envisaged that staff will be encouraged to initiate conversations in users' own spaces. This will involve supporting staff still further as they move out of their comfort zone of writing for Learning Services or their own blogs and Twitter accounts and begin responding to the blog posts and tweets of users.

Assess (again): measuring and describing Service impact
Using infographics to tell stories with data

Infographics, or using pictures to represent information, data or knowledge, have been used in the media for a number of years but are still, according to Giardina and Medina (2013), a relatively new concept in the digital world. Segel and Heer (2010) describe how the design of infographics can allow stories to be told using data. This is an emerging area where Learning Services, influenced by work undertaken by Harvard[6] and elsewhere[7] see many opportunities for communicating to their users the messages from otherwise dry or complex data. As storytelling is a means of user engagement and forms part of the customer-centred strategy, the Service is now using infographics to present survey and activity data back to users and other stakeholders in order to inform and to generate conversations with them about the Service.

Work on developing infographics began with publicizing the results of the 2012/13 student e-Learning survey discussed earlier. Whilst the survey is an important source of information about student use and expectations of University-provided technology, presenting dense and complex data as visually and as attractively as possible had proved a challenge within the limitations of text and spreadsheet graphics. Figure 3.5 is an infographic demonstrating increasing levels of satisfaction and interaction with the institutional VLE, which is also managed by Learning Services.

Figure 3.5 *Student survey data infographic*
Source: EHU (reproduced with permission)

The Service is also using infographics to attract attention by making its standard reporting to faculty and other University committees more visually appealing. The infographic in Figure 3.6 was used in a Learning Services update to faculty to communicate some interesting findings from a survey into students' views on reading lists. Infographics are being created wherever possible to convey quantitative information to users in multiple places; plasma screens across campus, web pages, reports and newsletters, the VLE and even as a searchable collection in their own right.[8]

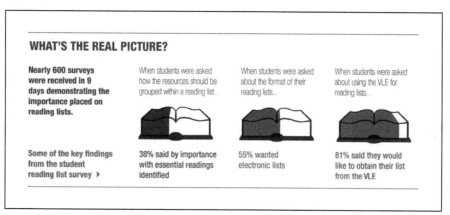

WHAT'S THE REAL PICTURE?

Nearly 600 surveys were received in 9 days demonstrating the importance placed on reading lists.

When students were asked how the resources should be grouped within a reading list…

When students were asked about the format of their reading lists…

When students were asked about using the VLE for reading lists…

Some of the key findings from the student reading list survey ▶

38% said by importance with essential readings identified

55% wanted electronic lists

81% said they would like to obtain their list from the VLE

Figure 3.6   *Infographic showing student reading list survey data*
   Source: Learning Services, Edge Hill University

Key performance indicators

Operating library services in a vacuum is never an option and as budgets are frequently constrained, strategic decisions on resource allocation must take into account what value or impact that particular resource use provides. Learning Services, along with academic libraries across the UK, has sought to operate within a relatively static budget by introducing technology to 'back-of-house' processes and some user activities over a number of years. The associated cost savings and efficiencies have made it possible to introduce new services, including the initiatives described in this chapter. However, these must at some point demonstrate real impact on customer satisfaction in order to remain viable.

The development of the Service's value statements has also informed work around the associated key performance indicators (KPIs) and metrics that measure performance. This joined-up activity will, it is hoped, ensure that the activities measured are those that connect with the customer experience, thus closing the loop. The three KPIs are as follows:

- *Customer Excellence: our product is high-quality support and resources*
  KPI – Learning Services is the go to place for study, support (physical and virtual) and resources
- *Operational Excellence: our operational systems and processes are customer-focused and effective*
  KPIs – The VLE is a core teaching and learning system; Learning Services provides value for money
- *Staff Engagement: our staff drive our customer and operational excellence improvements*
  KPIs – Staff are proud of the Service and willing to go the extra mile; Learning Services staff are engaged in academic liaison.

The metrics with which the Service has traditionally measured its performance are, at least on their own, not capable of measuring user engagement via digital media and consequent impact on user behaviour and satisfaction. A rethink of what is measured has been necessary in order to form a clear picture of how the new initiatives are progressing. Digital and social media generate activity data, so website and blog 'hits' are regarded as useful indicators of digital 'footfall', whereas 'likes', 'friends' and 'followers' provide an indication that users are at least reading the content. Comments and direct messages are considered to be indicators of a more reciprocal engagement with users, although it is recognized that measures of culture and user engagement can be difficult to quantify. The Service is beginning to triangulate this activity data against other measures – for example, data on resource use within disciplines – to see if it can ascertain evidence of changes in behaviour around resource use and in satisfaction with resources due to greater awareness of them.

A full academic year working with the KPIs has not been completed at the time of writing, and so it is not yet possible to discuss any measurable impact. It should be noted, however, that the process of developing them has brought something new to senior meetings and reinforced the idea that marketing and promotion is a shared management responsibility, along with data collection and performance measurement.

Conclusion

Digital technologies have enabled libraries to streamline operations and make efficiency savings in order to expand their services and move resources to where there is most benefit. The library is no longer an automatic first choice for users who increasingly inhabit a digital world but, in hanging on to past practices of 'selling' the library as a collection of books and related services, the diversity of what libraries do is invisible to users and other stakeholders. Instead, the library needs to engage with users to better understand their workflows and build their services around them.

This chapter has described the experience of Edge Hill University's Learning Services as it has sought to make the transition from a service-centred marketing approach to one that is customer-centred and which is understood and owned by all staff. Writing a value proposition has enabled the Service to articulate and share its core beliefs as an important first step in putting the customer before the product as a means of improving use of and satisfaction with library services. Two new marketing-related roles have been crucial in ensuring a consistent, Service-wide approach to ensure that all staff within the Service understand what is expected of them and why the changes are necessary.

Internal cultural change, website redesign, improving the digital skills of staff and having them change user perceptions by engaging with them in new ways was never going to be achieved quickly. This kind of change is an iterative process and much of it is in uncharted, digital territory. The Service continues to be in transition, although in using a customer-centred marketing approach as its compass it is going in the right direction.

Notes

1   www.edgehill.ac.uk/ls.
2   www.activitydata.org/index.html.
3   https://gcn.civilservice.gov.uk/guidance/customer-journey-mapping.
4   http://blogs.edgehill.ac.uk/ls.
5   http://blogs.edgehill.ac.uk/learningedge.
6   http://osc.hul.harvard.edu/sites/default/files/Analytics_Recommendations.pdf.
7   www.slideshare.net/CarliSpina/library-analytics-toolkit-14608730.
8   www.eshare.edgehill.ac.uk/3532.

References

Alcock, J. (2011) *Strategic Marketing in Academic Libraries: an examination of current practice*, MSc Econ dissertation, University of Aberystwyth, http://cadair.aber.ac.uk/dspace/bitstream/handle/2160/7732/jo%20alcock%20-%20strategic%20marketing%20in%20academic%20libraries.pdf?sequence=1.

Bury, R. and Phillips, M. (2008) Any Time, Any Place, Anywhere: a fresh approach to marketing at Edge Hill: marketing library services. In Brewerton, A. (ed.), *Marketing Library Services – a SCONUL working paper*, Society of College, National and University Libraries, London, 165–7.

Calder, C., Thaney, K. and Killingworth, S. (2013) *Breaking the Boundaries of Scholarly Publishing: the library perspective*, UKSG, www.slideshare.net/UKSG/calder-palgrave-uksg.

Dempsey, L. (2012) Libraries and the Informational Future: some notes. In Marchionini, G. and Moran, B. B. (eds), *Informational Professionals 2050: educational possibilities and pathways*, School of Information and Library Science, University of North Carolina at Chapel Hill, NC, http://sils.unc.edu/sites/default/files/publications/Information-Professionals-2050.pdf.

Estall, C. and Stephens, D. (2011) A Study of the Variables Influencing Academic Library Staff's Attitudes Toward Marketing, *New Review of Academic Librarianship*, **17**, 185–208.

Gall, D. (2010) Library Like a Rock Star: using your personal brand to promote your services and reach distant users, *Journal of Library Administration*, **50**, 628–37.

Giardina, M. and Medina, P. (2013) Information Graphics Design Challenges and Workflow Management, *Online Journal of Communication and Media Technologies*, **3** (1), 108–24.

Google and Ipsos (2012) *New Insights into Consumer Usage of Mobile Devices, the Shift to Smartphones and the Emergence of Tablets*, http://services.google.com/fh/files/blogs/Google_Ipsos_Mobile_Internet_Smartphone_Adoption_Insights_2011.pdf.

Gupta, D. K. (2002) What is Marketing in Libraries? Concepts, orientations, and practices, *Information Outlook: the monthly magazine of the Special Libraries Association*, **6** (11), 24–31.

Hagel III, J., Seely Brown, J. and Davison, L. (2010) *The Power of Pull: how small moves, smartly made, can set big things in motion*, Basic Books, New York, NY.

Housewright, R., Schonfield, R. C. and Wulfson, K. (2013) UK Survey of Academics 2012, Ithaka S+R, Jisc and RLUK, www.sr.ithaka.org/research-publications/ithaka-sr-jisc-rluk-uk-survey-academics-2012.

Kotler, P. and Andreasen, A. (1991) *Strategic Marketing for Non-profit Organizations*, 4th edn, Prentice Hall, Englewood Cliffs, NJ.

Martin, L. (2012) *The Fourth EHU Student Elearning Survey Headlines (2011/12)*, www.eshare.edgehill.ac.uk/1348.

Mathews, B. (2009) *Marketing Today's Academic Library: a bold new approach to communicating with students*, American Library Association, Chicago, IL.

Nunn, B. and Rouane, E. (2011) Marketing Gets Personal: promoting reference staff to reach users, *Journal of Library Administration*, **51**, 291–300.

RIN and SCONUL (2010) *Challenges for Academic Libraries in Difficult Economic Times: a guide for senior institutional managers and policy makers*, www.rin.ac.uk/system/files/attachments/Challenges-for-libraries-FINAL-March10.pdf.

Segel, E. and Heer, J. (2010) Narrative Visualization: telling stories with data, *IEEE Transactions on Visualization and Computer Graphics*, **16** (6), 1139–48.

Singh, R. (2009) Does Your Library Have an Attitude Problem Towards 'Marketing'? Revealing inter-relationship between marketing attitudes and behaviour, *Journal of Academic Librarianship*, **35** (1), 25–32.

THEME 2

Rethinking support for academic practice

The impact of open and digital content on librarians' roles in a learning and teaching context

Helen Howard

Introduction

This chapter focuses on the ways in which the open movement has impacted on librarians' roles in a learning and teaching context, primarily from a UK higher education perspective. Librarians and libraries have been influenced by and have had an impact on the open movement for many years, beginning with the provision and management of digital content in general, to specific activities around repositories for digitized and born-digital content and research outputs.

The move towards Open Educational Resources (OER) has resulted in a significant volume of high-quality open digital content, in addition to more general digital information and digitized resources, available free on the web. This presents two key opportunities for librarians involved in learning and teaching: first, to support and enable users to discover, reuse, manage, create and share learning and teaching resources in a global context; and second, as teachers and educators themselves, to participate in the OER movement by sharing their own teaching materials widely.

Background

OER are defined as 'teaching, learning or research materials that are in the public domain or released with an intellectual property licence that allows for free use, adaptation and distribution' (UNESCO, 2013). In summary, they can be large or small learning resources or tools, a whole course or a single file, with an open licence to be shared, edited, repurposed and reused by others. OER have become a global issue: UNESCO includes them as a priority under its 'access to knowledge' theme and maintains an OER community and toolkit. The recent European Commission document on education and skills identifies the potential of open learning and recommends that 'Europe should exploit the potential of OER much more than is currently the case' (European Commission, 2012, 9).

Some of the early examples of OER creation and sharing came from the USA. Firstly, MIT OpenCourseWare[1] (OCW) was launched in 2002 and then formed the basis of the OCW Consortium[2], an international group of educational institutions creating and releasing open content using a shared model. In the UK, the Open University[3] was one of the first universities to offer its resources free online in 2006, including tasters of its courses. Jisc activity in this area, particularly its recent OER programme with the Higher Education Academy (HEA) which supports the creation, use and promotion of OER and the continued use of Jorum[4] as an open national repository, demonstrate key UK higher education developments in this area. Recent developments and projects focus less on tools and technologies and more on strategy, policy and cultural change around open content. They are also moving increasingly towards addressing learning and teaching issues specifically, perhaps because work on institutional repositories in the mid-2000s had focused mainly on research outputs as opposed to learning and teaching resources (McGill, 2012, 3).

Benefits and uses of OER

Numerous institutions across the world now offer OER via in-house repositories, on websites, wikis, blogs and open virtual learning environments (VLEs), as well as in national repositories, such as MERLOT[5] and Jorum. Thus more than ten years on from the MIT OCW development, the OER movement continues to grow and become more mainstream. A recent study identifies that 'the use of digital resources to support teaching and learning in Higher Education (HE) is widespread and appears to be standard practice for the majority' (White and Manton, 2011, 1). Through discussions with academic staff, the study gathered information on how and why they use OER and revealed that 'reusing online content and resources is becoming increasingly normalised' (White and Manton, 2011, 10). Though this is due in part to factors such as the availability of licences, faster broadband and mobile and Web 2.0 technologies (Robertson, 2010), it is also due to the well documented benefits of OER use to both institutions and individual staff. In addition to having a positive impact on public image, reputation and marketing (D'Antoni, 2009, 6), an open approach can actually improve the quality of learning resources and teaching practices (McGill et al., 2008, 24; Nikoi, 2010, 17). Studies have shown that most academic staff reuse small resources to enhance their learning and teaching, with the aim of providing an improved, more engaging experience for learners, rather than to save time themselves (White and Manton, 2011, 12; Nikoi, 2010, 13).

From a student perspective, the use of OER is also seen as a positive thing. An international study of undergraduate students found that the majority wanted to see greater use of open content (57%), a significant rise on the response to the same question in the previous year (19%) (Dahlstrom, 2012, 12). Other surveys reveal that students consider that OER support background, independent learning and revision, in a flexible and accessible way (Nikoi, 2010, 13) and, when selected by academic staff, can help 'to steer them [students] through the potentially overwhelming volume of material online' (White and Manton, 2011, 1).

Librarians and OER

Kazakoff-Lane recognizes the role librarians have played in open access and the move towards OER: 'many in the profession have been strong, vocal advocates for Open Access and are starting to become cognizant of its curriculum equivalent: Open Educational Resources' (Kazakoff-Lane, 2012, 135). Graham and Secker also recognize this role for librarians. Their research found that 'librarians were obvious advocates for the OER movement and by sharing their own materials and developing systems to manage OERs, they could provide valuable advice and guidance to other teaching colleagues' (Graham and Secker, 2012, 2) .

A number of recent surveys and studies provide an insight into the different ways in which librarians are contributing to open educational developments in teaching and learning. They also highlight the gaps or opportunities where further input could prove beneficial. According to a report by Bueno-de-la-Fuente, Robertson and Boon, which examined the role of librarians in OER initiatives, their involvement is 'significant: three out of four projects teams count on at least one librarian' (Bueno-de-la-Fuente, Robertson and Boon, 2012, 1–2), with the main areas of involvement being 'description and classification, management, preservation, dissemination and promotion of OER' (Bueno-de-la-Fuente, Robertson and Boon, 2012, 2). However, outside specific project work, the study revealed a general lack of awareness and engagement on both sides; that is, from librarians engaging with OER, as well as a lack of understanding from those working within the OER area of the support which libraries could provide. The report identifies the need for librarians to develop expertise in supporting others to exploit OER, in particular in the areas of intellectual property rights, technologies, standards, licences and digital literacy skills. The authors identify a 'clear need of their (libraries) skills and knowledge (for example, advising and training about intellectual property and digital literacy)' (Bueno-de-la-Fuente, Robertson and Boon, 2012, 12).

These findings are borne out by responses gathered in the 2012 *SCORE Library Survey Report* (Support Centre for Open Resources in Education, 2012), which examined librarians' engagement with and experience of OER. The majority of librarians surveyed reported a lack of knowledge of Creative Commons (CC) licences and recognized this as a problem for potential OER creators and users as well. Of librarians surveyed, 69% were not currently involved in supporting academic staff to use OER, for example by providing training or advice, and requests for help with discovering OER for use in learning and teaching had been minimal. In relation to sharing their own teaching and learning materials, Graham and Secker found that librarians were keen to do so, but needed to improve their confidence and knowledge of OER practices. A lack of understanding of Creative Commons and licences in general was found to be a significant barrier to making content open, along with not knowing where to share materials or how to exploit repositories (Graham and Secker, 2012, 10).

As part of the Jisc Developing Digital Literacies programme, SCONUL (Society of College, National and University Libraries) surveyed senior staff from its member libraries to establish a picture of the digital literacy skills and capabilities of information professionals working in technology-rich environments and to consider how these roles might be more effective. Survey respondents reported high levels of expertise in information literacy, ICT and communication skills amongst their staff, but lower levels in digital scholarship and media literacy. Digital scholarship was described as 'the ability to participate in emerging academic, professional and research practices that depend on digital systems' (SCONUL, 2012) and included issues of open publication, licences and the repurposing of resources. Respondents considered 8% of information professionals 'experts' in this area and 44% 'novices'. In addition, a significant majority (77%) considered it essential for staff to develop capabilities in digital scholarship, thus identifying a gap between current understanding and skills and what will be needed in future to support users in digital scholarship and open educational practices.

Thus the evidence from surveys and reports suggests that librarians have a significant role to play within developments relating to open education but, in some cases, they currently lack the skills and expertise needed to contribute fully. In relation to OER, there are roles for librarians in both creating and sharing their own teaching and learning content, as well as providing advocacy and support for others to exploit OER to best advantage.

Supporting others in an open educational environment

This section looks at the roles and activities librarians are undertaking to support others in the creation and use of open and digital content. It examines the support needed by staff and students to undertake learning and teaching activities in a digital context, including being able to understand, assess, evaluate, use and manage a wide range of digital information.

Digital literacy skills of learners and teachers

Digital literacy, as defined by Jisc, encompasses 'those capabilities which fit an individual for living, learning and working in a digital society' (Jisc, 2013). In order to accommodate the continually changing ways of working and learning, there is a need for us all to be comfortable and flexible with digital technologies. This does not necessarily mean being familiar or competent with a large range of learning and teaching tools, but rather being able to evaluate and adopt different technologies or ways of working where necessary. In their work on learning literacies for the digital age, Beetham, McGill and Littlejohn (2009, 5) describe this as a need for 'adaptivity', 'agility' and 'confidence/exploration'. In line with many learning skills, digital literacy is not learnt once and never forgotten, but is constantly developing (Institute of Education, 2012).

There is evidence to suggest significant gaps in digital literacy skills amongst learners and teachers, a lack of awareness of the need for such skills and 'poor support for learners' developing strategies to make effective use of technologies for learning' (Beetham, McGill and Littlejohn, 2009, 4). A lack of digital literacy skills is a barrier to full engagement with OER and the ability to discover, evaluate, use and, where appropriate, adapt resources. Student use of online resources and digital technologies for learning is influenced by the teaching approaches of their lecturers (Margaryan, Littlejohn and Vojt, 2011; Beetham, McGill and Littlejohn, 2009), so professional development for teaching and support staff on the critical use of learning technologies and pedagogies for a digital age is particularly important (Jisc, 2010, 7).

For learners, the development of OER enables them to actively contribute and share their outputs in ways not previously possible. This follows the trend of students moving from consumers to producers of knowledge, but also raises issues about the skills needed for them to achieve this. Many learners struggle to translate skills they have with personal technologies to a learning context (Beetham, McGill and Littlejohn, 2009, 4). Furthermore, many students, even at postgraduate level, find the existing range of library databases and systems difficult to negotiate, highlighting a need to address basic information literacy skills in the digital environment (Institute of Education, 2012). An international survey of students in 2012 found that 'technology training and skill development for students is more important than new, more or "better" technology' (Dahlstrom, 2012, 5).

Librarians supporting digital literacy and OER developments

Traditionally, libraries manage and organize content, make it available and support learners in finding and using it. Given the range of quality information resources now available for free, particularly since the development of the open movement, librarians are recognizing the need to help staff and students develop an awareness of and ability to use digital content in all its forms. Library involvement in digital literacy skills development is widely recognized and is key to moving forward the open education agenda. Some examples of libraries supporting digital literacy skills development for learning and teaching are provided in the appendix to this chapter. In addition, a collection of case studies, including some from a library perspective, highlight digital literacy support, training and development for academic staff (Baume, 2013).

On a national level, SCONUL has developed lenses of its Seven Pillars of Information Literacy model for both digital literacy[6] and open content[7], in order to build understanding of these in a library context. As with the core Seven Pillars model (SCONUL, 2011), the new lenses have the potential to be used as a tool to underpin the development of knowledge and skills of staff, students and librarians.

In relation to OER developments, the Jisc-funded OpenStaffs project[8] was an early example of librarians supporting others to develop open content expertise. It aimed to enable the sharing and reuse of OER produced by academic staff, through the provision of an in-house repository and the availability of training and guidance. Libraries have also been involved in supporting open courses and more recently MOOCs (Massive Open Online Courses), particularly in areas such as copyright and metadata. For example, Leiden University Libraries support open courseware pilots through assisting with the provision of reading lists and online course readings, such as journal articles. In terms of MOOCs, Butler (2012, 2) reports that, in the USA, libraries have been most involved in supporting these in two key ways: by helping academic staff identify appropriate resources to support learning and 'to navigate the copyright issues raised by teaching in the open, online environment'.

Case study of an institutional approach to OER

This case study, based on work at the University of Leeds (UK), outlines the involvement of library staff in the development of an institutional OER policy (see Figure 4.1) and the areas of support required from the library to take forward its implementation.

Prior to 2012, the University of Leeds did not have an institutional policy or strategy in developing OER. Individual academic and support staff had been creating learning objects and, in some cases, sharing these openly on websites or in repositories, but there was little support or guidance institutionally. The University had significantly developed its systems for research outputs, establishing a shared White Rose Repository with the Universities of York and Sheffield, but had not considered the potential of housing and sharing teaching and learning resources as OER. In 2011, the University successfully bid for funds from the Jisc/HEA phase 3 OER programme to find ways of embedding OER within teaching and learning, by developing an institutional strategy, exploring the potential of OER with academic staff and producing a series of case studies of individual practitioner use.

The Leeds project ran a number of workshops with academic staff to investigate issues around OER in more detail. The findings were consistent with those reported by other surveys and studies (as mentioned above). Staff appreciated the potential benefits of OER but identified copyright issues, a lack of knowledge of Creative Commons licences and not having sufficient technical skills or learning technologist support as potential barriers to their creation and use (Morris, 2012a). The most significant concern, however, was

---

UNIVERSITY OF LEEDS

OPEN EDUCATIONAL RESOURCES

This document sets out the University's position and guidance on the use and publication of Open Educational Resources (OERs) within educational situations at the University.[1] It was endorsed by the Vice Chancellor's Executive Group and the Taught Student Education Board (as TSEB/12-15) in November 2012.

Background

1. The University strategy is to provide students with an exceptional student experience centred on inspirational learning and teaching.

2. The University is committed to a blended learning strategy which includes within relevant disciplinary contexts realising the potential for transformation: in terms of course design, methods, and students "engagement with learning material by a considered and appropriate mixture of face-to-face interaction, carefully designed online course materials and tools, and enhanced contact with a wider distributed learning environment through relevant technologies".[2]

3. Staff use a wide range of self-generated teaching materials to support exceptional teaching, including teaching notes, hand-outs, audio, images, animations, multimedia materials and others.

Figure 4.1   *Extract from the University of Leeds OER policy* [9]
Source: University of Leeds (reproduced with permission)

'the difficulty of locating suitable OERs in a reasonable timeframe' (Morris, 2012a, 2). The final project report lists areas of support requested by staff, including guidance on both producing and using OER, in particular clear advice on copyright and IPR issues in both areas (Morris, 2012b, 8).

As a result of the project, the University aims to create an OER 'portal', incorporating an institutional repository and support for OER use, including examples of best practice, licence information and key contacts. Whilst the project has been managed by staff from the Faculty of Biological Sciences and the Staff and Departmental Development Unit, library staff have supported the project in a number of ways. Initially, the library's copyright officer, VLE team leader and e-learning adviser joined the project steering group and contributed expertise in CC licences, use of national repositories and technical solutions. Perhaps more significantly, the library is now involved in the implementation group taking forward the institutional strategy and is considered as an area of the University ready to contribute learning objects to an institutional repository once established.

As the final project report outlines, it is hoped that lessons learnt from the Leeds project 'will be of use and benefit to other institutions which seek to develop similar policies and / or increase the creation, sharing and usage of

OERs in their institution' (Morris, 2012b, 9). In terms of outcomes for the library, the project has revealed a number of clear roles within institutional OER support which may well be common to many institutions. These roles are:

- copyright and IPR advice
- training for staff on both producing and using OER (in collaboration with the Staff and Departmental Development Unit)
- contribution of teaching resources to an institutional portal
- assistance with the development of a repository, in terms of technical and strategic advice
- advice and guidelines for students on producing and sharing their own OER.

These roles reinforce the need for libraries to have the capacity to offer support in a variety of areas and for different activities. They represent a broadening of traditional library roles, as well as the need for multi-skilled teams.

As well as establishing an institutional repository, the policy implementation involves engaging academic and support staff with the concept of OER and inviting them to consider how OER creation and use could impact on them. A series of events and activities are taking place to promote the agenda internally. Staff attending one event considered what practical strategies would enable them to embed OER in their learning and teaching. They suggested that seeing a collection of good-practice examples of usage and creation, in specific disciplines if possible, would be beneficial, perhaps highlighting the need to see the concept in action. Staff also required practical support in OER creation, relating to copyright, technologies and channels for publication. Finally, they recognized the need to build a culture of sharing internally, as well as externally, potentially with 'champions' to encourage, promote and provide examples of OER.

It is too early to say if an institutional policy such as this one will lead to an increase in the creation and use of OER or whether it will formalize the 'under the radar' sharing of materials and reuse of resources which already exists. The institutional approach can remove certain barriers to OER use, such as a lack of support, guidance and practical help and can significantly raise awareness amongst staff in particular. It should also lead to a more directed student use of good quality OER. However, this approach requires significant continued input in the form of advocacy, promotion and support, as well as training and development activities. ▨

Librarians as creators and users of OER

This section looks at the role of librarians as content creators, sharing their own resources and materials and at how they can support each other to achieve this. Librarians are creating, using and sharing OER to support their learning and teaching activities, particularly in the area of academic, information and digital literacies.

The ANimated Tutorial Sharing Project (ANTS)[10] was an early example of librarians working together to share OER. The project aimed to create and make openly available a large number of online multimedia learning objects. Through a collaboration of librarians from across Canada, the project provides OER for a wide range of information literacy topics. The collaborators agreed what resources were needed, initially to support distance learners, and created many of these themselves, as well as collecting resources from other librarians. Kazakoff-Lane recognizes the benefits of a shared resource in terms of efficiency: 'ANTS provides librarians with all the infrastructure they need to rationalize development, share files and support point-of-need content' (Kazakoff-Lane, 2012, 135). She also reflects that projects like ANTS facilitate the use of OER and therefore influence librarians towards greater awareness and appreciation of such resources.

Similar projects and initiatives have developed over the last few years in the UK as well, often involving smaller collaborations or single institutions. Examples of these include the BRUM Project (Birmingham Re-Usable Materials), which created a suite of reusable learning objects for information skills development, and Cardiff University's Information Literacy Resource Bank,[11] which makes available a range of online materials for reuse within and beyond Cardiff. In addition, Leeds University Library's Lecturer pages[12] provide teaching materials, including lesson plans, Powerpoints and handouts for both face-to-face and online learning on academic skills and information literacy topics for adaptation and reuse. Finally, the recent Jisc/HEA DELILA project[13] (Developing Educators Learning and Information Literacies for Accreditation) was established to find ways of embedding learning resources for information and digital literacy into teaching training within higher education.

Case study of an OER Community of Practice

Building on some of these initiatives, a co-ordinated approach to sharing digital and information literacy materials is being taken by Project CoPILOT (Community of Practice for Information Literacy Online Teaching)[14] funded initially by Jisc/HEA and managed by the University of Birmingham and London School of Economics, in partnership with the Information Literacy (IL) section of UNESCO. Whilst based in the UK, it aims to promote sharing of OER internationally by building a community of practice. Through a survey of librarians and an open workshop, results of the initial project research revealed that librarians were positive about sharing resources and familiar with doing this 'in a closed way', whilst 'open sharing is something many aspire to' (Graham and Secker, 2012, 11). Project research also showed that empowering and enabling librarians to openly share would take more than simply establishing a repository for teaching materials, as this in effect already exists through initiatives such as Jorum. Practical support and training would be needed to build awareness, knowledge and confidence within the library community.

The community of practice approach has been a successful model for resource sharing, particularly where collaboration already exists and services beyond the content itself are offered (McGill et al., 2008, 15). Through its community of practice, Project CoPILOT aims to provide support and training for librarians, in areas such as CC licences, design and pedagogy of OER and the adaptation of OER. In addition, it is enabling ongoing debate and discussion, as well as the sharing of materials, through an online community platform hosted by UNESCO (see Figure 4.2). The project leads initially used the platform to engage with librarians internationally, inviting them to contribute to various activities and discussions relating to OER (Graham and Secker, 2013).

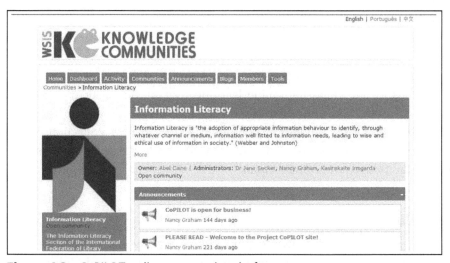

Figure 4.2 *CoPILOT online community platform*
Source: Project CoPILOT (reproduced with permission)

As well as practical support, through its advocacy and promotion of OER to the library community, Project CoPILOT is highlighting the potential for librarians to be active creators and users of OER in their own right, as well as acting as champions within their institutions, supporting colleagues in OER use and creation. The project has established a UK special interest group reporting to the Information Literacy Group of CILIP (The Chartered Institute of Library and Information Professionals), thus linking it into the broader IL agenda in the UK and benefiting from the support of a professional body. The project highlights the need for librarians to be engaged and active in these areas in order to drive forward the agenda, with key roles in advocacy and promotion, as well as the practical organization and management of an online community of practice and discussion list.

Digitized content for learning and teaching

Librarians have also had a role in making content held by their libraries openly available for learning and teaching purposes, particularly relating to rare or unique collections. This has the benefit of making historical materials available to a wider audience, though most initiatives are not developed with the aim of allowing users to adapt and repurpose the materials. Examples of this open approach include Harvard University Open Collections Program,[15] which has created a series of online collections on different topics through the digitization of the library's historical materials and manuscripts, with the addition of commentary and explanation for teaching and learning purposes.

Smaller-scale examples also exist in the UK. The Jisc-funded Scarlet project[16] (Special Collections using Augmented Reality to enhance Learning and Teaching) at the University of Manchester Library brings original materials to life, alongside online learning content. Similarly, the Literary Archive project[17] at Leeds University Library aims to produce a range of teaching resources combining content from its special collections with detailed commentary to show the development of different forms of literature from draft to final version.

Conclusion

Open education has grown significantly over the last ten years and continues to do so, with OER becoming more prominent and high profile. Most recently, the popularity of MOOCs, which allow anyone to sign up for an online course without being formally enrolled at the institution, demonstrates this continuing trend. The current evidence suggests that whilst the use of open content is widespread and beneficial to institutions, teachers and learners, the lack of digital literacy skills (particularly those of academic staff) and understanding of open content issues are preventing the full exploitation of digital resources and OER in particular. The case studies outlined here describe different approaches to removing the practical barriers to promoting the use and creation of OERs. It is perhaps too early to say to what extent developments such as these will have a significant impact on individuals and institutions nationally.

The role of librarians in supporting others to develop the skills and knowledge needed in relation to OER is growing, but there is a continued need to promote ways in which their involvement can be beneficial. In addition, libraries may need to acknowledge the wide range of professional roles and skills required within a changing environment and move towards both a broadening of traditional library roles, as well as the creation of multi-professional teams. The case studies and examples of practice given here demonstrate the ability of librarians to have an impact on OER developments, at institutional, national and international levels. Indeed, the International Association of Universities identifies librarians as 'best placed to start the drive towards an increased involvement of their institutions in the OER movement' and goes so far as suggesting that being involved in OER activities 'could be a way to revive and adapt their role to the requirements of higher education today' (International Association of Universities, 2012, 2). However, librarians themselves recognize key areas around open content where they need to develop greater expertise, particularly if they are to take a lead in these developments. Addressing these areas will also enable librarians to make further progress in creating, sharing, using and adapting open content for their own learning and teaching activities.

Appendix – examples of library digital literacy initiatives

Edge Hill University's Learning Services runs a Digital Excellence staff development programme, including events for the 'digital practitioner' to build skills and understanding around the use of digital technologies in learning and teaching.

The Jisc-funded Digidol project at Cardiff University has produced a knowledge hub relevant to both staff and students that maps academic practices to digital tools and resources available: http://cmapspublic3. ihmc.us/rid=1KY550GR7-1YNJ9RF-CYP5/overview.html.

The Digital Dates programme at the University of Leeds offers short, informal workshops provided by and open to both staff and students to develop digital skills to support all aspects of University work: www.sddu. leeds.ac.uk/sddu-digital-dates.html.

Open University Library Services have developed a digital literacy framework which highlights the skills and knowledge needed at different levels of study: www.open.ac.uk/libraryservices/subsites/dilframework. Librarians also provide a guide for academic staff to build understanding of digital literacy, its significance and impact on learning and teaching, and to promote the embedding of related skills in the curriculum. For students, Being Digital, a set of online learning resources, is designed to support use of digital tools for study and work: www.open.ac.uk/libraryservices/ beingdigital.

The Digital Society programme provided by the University of Manchester Library is open to students from across the university and explores the impact of digital media and online technologies on different aspects of life and what it means to be a citizen in the digital world: www.college. manchester.ac.uk/courses/semester2/thedigitalsociety.

Glossary

CILIP: the Chartered Institute of Library and Information Professionals – professional body for UK librarians.

HEA: Higher Education Academy – national organization supporting learning and teaching in UK higher education.

ICT: Information and communications technology.

IL: Information literacy.

IPR: Intellectual property rights.

Jisc: (formerly JISC, the Joint Information Systems Committee) – national organization promoting the use of digital technologies in UK further and higher education.

Jorum: UK-based national online repository for further and higher education learning and teaching materials.

MERLOT: Multimedia Educational Resource for Learning and Online Teaching – US-based national online repository of learning and teaching materials.

MIT: Massachusetts Institute of Technology.

MOOC: Massive open online course – free educational courses available on
   the internet.
OER: Open educational resources.
SCONUL: Society of College, National and University Libraries – national
   organization representing UK libraries.
SCORE: Support Centre for Open Resources in Education – UK-based
   project supporting OER use.
UNESCO: United Nations Educational, Scientific and Cultural Organization.
VLE : Virtual learning environment.

Notes

1   http://ocw.mit.edu/index.htm.
2   www.ocwconsortium.org.
3   www.open.edu/openlearn.
4   www.jorum.ac.uk.
5   www.merlot.org/merlot/index.htm.
6   www.sconul.ac.uk/publication/digital-literacy-lens.
7   www.sconul.ac.uk/publication/oer-lens.
8   www.jisc.ac.uk/whatwedo/programmes/elearning/oer/openstaffs.aspx.
9   http://dspace.jorum.ac.uk/xmlui/handle/123456789/17559.
10 http://ants.wetpaint.com.
11 https://ilrb.cf.ac.uk.
12 http://library.leeds.ac.uk/skills-lecturers.
13 http://delilaopen.wordpress.com.
14 http://delilaopen.wordpress.com/project-co-pilot.
15 http://ocp.hul.harvard.edu.
16 http://teamscarlet.wordpress.com.
17 http://library.leeds.ac.uk/tutorials/manuscripts/graham-greene.
    http://library.leeds.ac.uk/tutorials/manuscripts/geoffrey-hill.

References

Baume, D. (ed.) (2013) Case Studies. In *JISC & Professional Associations Guide to
   Implementing the UK Professional Standards Framework in the Digital University*,
   http://jiscdesignstudio.pbworks.com/w/file/62730732/Case%20Studies_2.docx.
Beetham, H., McGill, L. and Littlejohn, A. (2009) *Thriving in the 21st Century:
   learning literacies for the Digital Age (LLiDA project): executive summary, conclusions
   and recommendations*,

www.jisc.ac.uk/media/documents/projects/llidaexecsumjune2009.pdf.

Bueno-de-la-Fuente, G., Robertson, R. J. and Boon, S. (2012) *The Roles of Libraries and Information Professionals in Open Educational Resources (OER) Initiatives,* Survey report, CAPLE/Jisc CETIS, http://publications.cetis.ac.uk/2012/492.

Butler, B. (2012) *Massive Open Online Courses: legal and policy issues for research libraries,* Issue Brief, Association of Research Libraries, www.arl.org/storage/documents/publications/issuebrief-mooc-22oct12.pdf.

Dahlstrom, E. (2012) *ECAR Study of Undergraduate Students and Information Technology, 2012,* (Research Report), EDUCAUSE Center for Applied Research.

D'Antoni, S. (2009) Open Educational Resources: reviewing initiatives and issues, *Open Learning: the Journal of Open, Distance and e-Learning,* **24** (1), 3–10.

European Commission (2012) *Rethinking Education: investing in skills for better socio-economic outcomes,* COM (12)669, final.

Graham, N. and Secker, J. (2012) *Librarians, Information Literacy and Open Educational Resources: report of a survey,*
http://delilaopen.files.wordpress.com/2012/04/findingsharingoers_reportfinal1.pdf.

Graham, N. and Secker, J. (2013) *Project CoPILOT: community of practice for information literacy online teaching: a case study of an international online community,* The Higher Education Academy,
http://delilaopen.files.wordpress.com/2013/03/bham-final.pdf.

Institute of Education (2012) *Digital Literacy as a Postgraduate Attribute*? Interim report,
www.jisc.ac.uk/media/documents/programmes/elearning/DL%20Interim%20Report%20IOE%20Diglits%20IOE%20interim%20report%20Aug%2012.pdf.

International Association of Universities (2012) *Training and Support Programme for Academic Librarians on OER Use, Reuse and Production,* IAU-OER Concept Note, www.iau-aiu.net/sites/all/files/OER_Concept%20Note_2.doc.

Jisc (2010) *Supporting Learners in a Digital Age (SLiDA) Synthesis Report,*
www.jisc.ac.uk/media/documents/programmes/elearning/slidasynthesisreport.pdf.

Jisc (2013) *Developing Digital Literacies,* www.jisc.ac.uk/developingdigitalliteracies.

Kazakoff-Lane, C. (2012) Moving Information Literacy Beyond Library 2.0: multimedia, multi-device, point-of-need screencasts via the ANimated Tutorial Sharing Project. In Godwin, P. and Parker, J. (eds), *Information Literacy beyond Library 2.0,* Facet Publishing, London.

Margaryan, A., Littlejohn, A. and Vojt, G. (2011) Are Digital Natives a Myth or Reality? University students' use of digital technologies, *Computers and Education,* **56** (2), 429–40.

McGill, L. (2012) Open Educational Resources Timeline, *Other Voices blog,* 13 February, http://blogs.cetis.ac.uk/othervoices/2012/02/13/open-educational-resources-timeline.

McGill, L., Currier, S., Duncan, C. and Douglas, P. (2008) *Good Intentions: improving the evidence base in support of sharing learning materials,* http://repository.jisc.ac.uk/265.

Morris, N. (2012a) *Recommendations for Increasing Engagement with Open Educational Resources,* Report to the Blended Learning Steering Group, University of Leeds.

Morris, N. (2012b) *Embedding Open Educational Resources into Student Education Institutionally,* HEA/Jisc final report, www.heacademy.ac.uk/projects/detail/oer/OER_COM2_Leeds.

Nikoi, S. (2010) *Open Transferable Technology-Enabled Educational Resources (OTTER) Project: stakeholder views on open educational resources,* Research Report, University of Leicester, www2.le.ac.uk/departments/beyond-distance-research-alliance/ projects/otter/documentation/researchreport.pdf.

Robertson, J. (2010) Libraries, Librarians and Open Educational Resources, *John's JISC CETIS blog,* 9 February, http://blogs.cetis.ac.uk/johnr/2010/02/09/libraries-librarians-and-open-educational-resources.

SCONUL (2011) *The SCONUL Seven Pillars of Information Literacy Model,* www.sconul.ac.uk/sites/default/files/documents/coremodel.pdf.

SCONUL (2012) *Summary Report on Baseline Survey of Digital Literacy,* www.sconul.ac.uk/sites/default/files/documents/Digital_Literacies_Baseline_ survey_summary.pdf.

Support Centre for Open Resources in Education (2012) *SCORE Library Survey Report,* www.open.ac.uk/score/files/score/file/Library%20Survey% 20Report%20final%2014022012.pdf.

UNESCO (2013) *Open Educational Resources,* www.unesco.org/new/en/communication-and-information/access-to-knowledge/ open-educational-resources.

White, D. and Manton, M. (2011) *Open Educational Resources: the value of reuse in higher education,* OER Impact Study Report, University of Oxford, www.jisc.ac.uk/media/documents/programmes/elearning/oer/ OERTheValueOfReuseInHigherEducation.pdf.

CHAPTER 5

Supporting early-career researchers in data management and curation

Joy Davidson

Introduction

While scholarly publishing remains the key means for determining researchers' impact, international funding body requirements and government recommendations relating to research data management (RDM), sharing and preservation mean that the underlying research data is becoming increasingly valuable in its own right. This is true not only for researchers in the sciences but also in the humanities and creative arts as well. The ability to exploit their own and others' data is emerging as a crucial skill for researchers across all disciplines. However, despite early-career researchers being 'highly competent and ubiquitous users of information technologies generally' there appears to be a widespread lack of understanding and uncertainty about open access and self-archiving across the research communities (Jisc, 2013).

This changing landscape will impact most keenly upon academic libraries over the next few years as they work with infrastructure and support systems to identify and maintain access to an array of research data outputs. Taking a largely UK perspective and drawing upon the work of the Digital Curation Centre (DCC),[1] a centre of expertise in digital curation, this chapter will explore some of the background to what is currently a shifting research data landscape. It will provide a context for examining the role of the library as part of institutional infrastructure and consider how academic librarians might support early-career researchers.

Building shared understandings: research data, its management and curation

Shared concepts of what comprises research data, its management and curation are essential for ensuring that researchers are able to adhere to institutional and funding body policies and mandates. This section aims to explore the key concepts, practices and drivers relating to RDM from the library and librarian perspective.

Librarians need to understand what research data might include

Determining exactly what is meant by the term research data and what sorts of research outputs need to be considered is an ongoing challenge. Definitions vary across disciplines, funders and publishers. For anyone working to support researchers in managing and sharing their data within a higher education institution (HEI), it is essential that a clearly defined view of what constitutes research data is agreed early and endorsed at the right levels: research group, school, college, university-wide.

As a general guide, the DCC recommends that researchers should consider how they will maintain access to any research data that may be necessary for enabling the validation of their published research findings. By way of example, the University of Glasgow's research data is defined as: 'any material (digital or physical) required to underpin research. For different disciplines this may include raw data captured from instruments, derived data, documents, spreadsheets & databases, lab notebooks, visualisations, models, software, images, measurements and numbers' (University of Glasgow, 2012).

While the term research data is something that the majority of science, technology, engineering and mathematics (STEM) researchers are comfortable with as a description of their academic outputs, many researchers in the arts do not see themselves as data producers. There are, however, ongoing efforts to better define research data for arts researchers; for example, the University of the Creative Arts London policy states that non-digital materials such as sketch books are covered in their RDM Policy. Research being undertaken by DCC staff in collaboration with the Jisc-funded KAPTUR project at the University of the Creative Arts has also helped to illuminate other possible definitions for research data outputs within the arts:

'documenting the research process' & 'visualisation and documentation' were offered as alternatives to research data. . . . Idea of 'organisational moments' or 'trigger points for data creation or management activity'.

Guy et al., 2013

Whatever an institution's definition of research data outputs, librarians need to understand these definitions so they can explain them to researchers as and when needed.

Understanding the range of RDM and curation activities

Once institutions have reached agreement on what they consider to be research data, the next step is to identify what support will be needed to ensure that this data is actively managed and curated as required by funder and publisher mandates, as well as institutional policies. The DCC defines curation as 'the active management and appraisal of data over the lifecycle of scholarly and scientific interest' (DCC, n.d.). Data management and curation involves many stakeholders, including IT and library staff, research administrators and senior managers. It will be crucial that these varied stakeholders communicate effectively with each other and understand their roles and responsibilities in supporting RDM and the sharing of data. The DCC developed the Curation Lifecycle Model (Higgins, 2008) to help break down the wide range of curation activities so that specific roles and responsibilities can be identified and assigned. Having data at its core, the model can assist institutions to articulate and refine research workflows and to develop support services that enable the wide range of stakeholders involved to meet data management and curation requirements.

The model focuses on nine key areas of activity, ranging from conceiving new research projects through to providing longer-term access and facilitating reuse. These actions are depicted in the outer ring of the model (see Figure 5.1 on the next page). The model is cyclical in nature and it should be noted that users may engage with the model at any stage, not necessarily at the outset of new research activity – the conceptualization stage – which is the notional ideal. In reality, there will probably be many cases where management and curation are not considered until the point of ingestion into a repository and repository staff will then need to work back through the model to identify additional contextual information needed to make the data accessible and reusable. Furthermore, as data-driven science becomes more commonplace, researchers may begin the curation lifecycle at the 'transform' stage by accessing and reusing others' data to lead to new research questions.

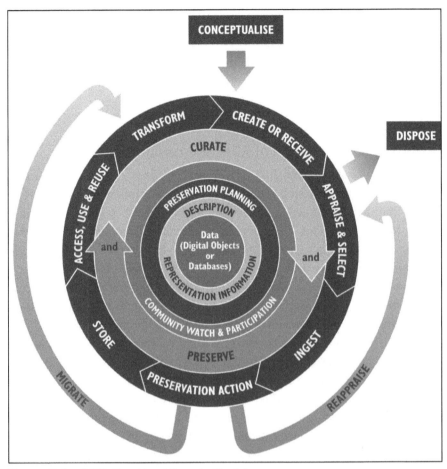

Figure 5.1   *DCC's Curation Lifecycle Model*
    Source: Digital Curation Centre (reproduced with permission)

Librarians already have a role to play in ingesting, storing and providing access to research data that is deposited by researchers. However, by seeking to become more involved during the grant application and active research phases, librarians need to be in an informed position to help researchers plan for increased access and use of their research outputs by making them more visible and understandable to external users.

Drivers for change
RDM, data curation and the international context

In recent years, RDM and the sharing of data have emerged as key themes in a number of countries worldwide. In 2007, the Organisation for Economic Co-operation and Development (OECD) declared that it viewed research data as a public good (OECD, 2007). Since then, a number of funding bodies in the USA and UK have mandated that data management plans be submitted at the grant proposal stage to ensure that data generated through publicly funded research will be accessible and reusable over time – usually a period of at least ten years. In the USA, the National Science Foundation (NSF) and National Institutes for Health (NIH) have been mandating data management plans be submitted with grant applications since 2009. From 2013, the NSF will also have the following requirements:

> For all new grant applications from 14 January, the US National Science Foundation (NSF) asks a principal investigator to list his or her research 'products' rather than 'publications' in the biographical sketch section. This means that, according to the NSF, a scientist's worth is not dependent solely on publications. Data sets, software and other non-traditional research products will count too.
> Piwowar, 2013, 2

The inclusion of research products as part of a researcher's biographical sketch is an encouraging development and hopefully will be an approach that is considered by UK funders in the near future. In Europe, Horizon 2020[2] has made open access to research outputs a key objective. Indeed, it is likely that data management plans will be required as part of funding applications in the European Commission's FP8 programme. A number of high-profile reports have examined the need for improved infrastructure and research data management skills in the European landscape (Riding the Wave, European Union, 2010; Surfboard for Riding the Wave, Knowledge Exchange, 2011). Australia has invested heavily in developing and progressing a national approach to research data management through the establishment of the Australian National Data Service (ANDS). Canada established Research Data Canada in 2011 to formalize a national approach to supporting research data management and sharing. However, some of the most dramatic advances in the past two years have been seen in the UK. In 2010, Research Councils UK (RCUK) issued their Common Principles on Research Data Policy (RCUK, 2010) and subsequently individual RCUK funding bodies have mandated management of and access to publicly

funded research outputs, resulting in a flurry of activity in UK higher
education institutions to bolster their infrastructure to support RDM.

Case study: UK funders' requirements driving data management and sharing

Since Research Councils UK (RCUK) released its Common Principles on Data Policy
the majority of RCUK funders have mandated the inclusion of data management
plans with new grant applications. This approach places the responsibility on
individual researchers to provide evidence that data management and sharing
issues have been considered from the earliest stage of research activity.
However, the RCUK funding body Engineering and Physical Sciences Research
Council (EPSRC) has taken a different approach, with the release of their policy
framework in March 2011 that outlines nine expectations relating to research
data management and sharing for all UK HEIs seeking EPSRC funding (EPSRC,
2011). The expectations are aimed at HEIs rather than the researchers they
employ, thereby shifting the onus for providing evidence of research data
management and sharing infrastructure to the institution rather than the
researcher. EPSRC requested that HEIs produce roadmaps outlining how they will
meet these expectations by 1 May 2012 and expect institutions to be able to
comply fully with these expectations by 1 May 2015. The EPSRC expectations
have been a significant catalyst for assessing, developing and implementing
research data management support systems and have been instrumental for
getting the attention of senior management and budget holders.

In addition to expectations related to the management and retention of
research data, funders in the UK are increasingly advocating making both
research publications and research data openly accessible through gold open
access (OA) journals. This is clearly evident in the recent changes to the RCUK
policy on open access (RCUK, 2012), which states that:

> Peer reviewed research papers which result from research that is wholly or partially
> funded by the Research Councils:
>
> 1 must be published in journals which are compliant with Research Council policy on
>   Open Access (see section 4).
> 2 must include details of the funding that supported the research and a statement
>   on how the underlying research materials – such as data, samples or models – can
>   be accessed.
>
> RCUK, 2012

How publishers are influencing change

Most publishers have offered authors the option of submitting supplementary material such as data along with their publications for some time. However, publishers are increasingly mandating that underlying data be made available both to peer reviewers and upon request by subsequent readers of the article. Access to the underlying data facilitates validation of the research findings by peers but also enables reuse. The following excerpt from the journal *Nature*'s policy on the availability of data and materials[3] illustrates how data should be retained and also implies that the editors expect data to be described sufficiently to allow for validation and ease of reuse:

> An inherent principle of publication is that others should be able to replicate and build upon the authors' published claims. Therefore, a condition of publication in a *Nature* journal is that authors are required to make materials, data and associated protocols promptly available to readers without undue qualifications

Nature further reserves the right to refuse publication to authors who fail to provide evidence that they are able to comply with the journal's requirements for data sharing. Most recently, FigShare[4] joined up with Public Library of Science (PLOS)[5] in an effort to make the underlying data more readily accessible to 'enable researchers to do more with the data behind the papers, improving the transparency of the research and aid reproducibility' (Digital Science, 2013). However, many researchers still feel unsure about what data they need to make available.

Some benefits associated with research data management

Unsurprisingly, compliance with funders', institutions' and publishers' policies is not always the best incentive for motivating researchers to spend time on undertaking data management activities, which could otherwise be spent on research. Heather Piwowar, co-founder of the not-for-profit organization ImpactStory[6], has been carrying out research into the links between making data available and citations and more recently into altmetrics. Her research has revealed that researchers who share well managed and curated data can expect an increase of up to 69% in the number of citations they receive compared with those who do not (Piwowar, Day and Fridsma, 2007). Citations have a direct impact on researchers' career advancement and international standing. With regard to altmetrics, Piwowar states:

> In the next five years, I believe that it will become routine to track – and to value – citations to an online lab notebook, contributions to a software library, bookmarks to data sets from content-sharing sites such as Pinterest and Delicious. In other words, to value a wider range of metrics that suggest a research product has made a difference. For example, my colleagues and I have estimated that the data sets added to the US National Center for Biotechnology Information's Gene Expression Omnibus in 2007 have contributed to more than 1,000 papers. Such attributions continue to accumulate for several years after data sets are first made publicly available.
>
> Piwowar, 2013, 159

Over the past few years there has also been a marked increase in the number of data journals available to researchers such as GigaScience[7] and PANGAEA[8]. These journals offer an additional means of making research outputs accessible and, more importantly, citable.

The role of librarians in this emerging RDM landscape

So where do librarians fit within this changing context? This chapter now turns to an assessment of the role of libraries and librarians in supporting research and data management at all levels of their institution.

Developing institutional research data policies

As discussed earlier in the chapter, a number of drivers are making research data management and sharing a big priority for UK HEIs. Indeed, the EPSRC requirements on data management saw a flurry of RDM activity within UK HEIs over the 2012–13 period, with most seeking to develop and implement policies and support services to underpin research data management and sharing. Encouragingly, the JISCMRD (Jisc Managing Research Data programme) projects[9] and the first tranche of DCC institutional engagements (IEs) reveal that many UK HEIs are looking to their libraries not just to participate in, but to lead on, the development and implementation of these policies and related support services. What has also been learnt is that before an institution can develop policies or support services that are fit for purpose, reflect working practice and, most crucially, achieve buy-in from researchers, it is imperative they obtain an in-depth understanding of current research workflows for different research units and disciplines and an understanding of their data holdings.

Baselining institutional RDM practices using the Data Asset Framework (DAF)

The Data Asset Framework (DAF) is a freely available survey and interview-based methodology and provides access to a number of sample questionnaires and interview questions. DAF is a useful means of assessing how much data is being generated within an institution and how it is being managed. DAF has been used by a number of the JISCMRD projects and has been used as a starting point in most of the DCC institutional engagements.The Jisc-funded Open Exeter project[10] is a good example of RDM policy development and service provision being led by library staff. The Open Exeter project adapted the DAF questionnaires as part of their 'Follow the Data' work and succeeded in getting over 280 respondents from across the institution to feed back on their current research data management and sharing practices. This has provided a sound basis for the project to identify where additional support is needed and how best to implement their research data policy.

Reviewing what other institutions are doing

A growing number of UK HEIs have made their research data policies and EPSRC roadmaps available via the DCC website.[11,12] These can also be an excellent starting point for any institution wishing to get an idea of what a policy relating to research data might comprise, as well as tips on how these policies might be implemented and supported. The DCC is also in the final stages of developing a practical how-to guide on setting up and delivering institutional research data management services which will provide case studies based on the JISCMRD projects and the DCC IEs.

Identifying researcher support needs

Since 2011 the DCC has been working with 21 UK HEIs to help them identify the skills and capability gaps within their institutions and to develop and implement research data management policies, support services and infrastructure. Based on the outcomes of the initial strand of engagements, it has become clear that libraries are leading the development and delivery of research data management services in many UK HEIs. Indeed, if the ultimate return on investment for managing, sharing and curating research data is to realize data reuse and ultimately increase the body of scholarly knowledge, libraries have a potentially crucial role to play in facilitating data discovery, contextualization, assessment and reuse.

Identifying where researchers most need support across the curation lifecycle and the best means of providing that support have been explored through a number of JISCMRD and RDM Training Materials (JISC RDMTrain) projects.[13] The DaMaRO project at the University of Oxford[14] recently undertook a survey of researchers in the sciences to find out where they need support most urgently:

> Perhaps unsurprisingly, the tasks in which most training had been received were those relating to day-to-day management of information: managing bibliographic data; organizing and structuring data within files; storing data securely and backing up; and organizing, structuring and naming files and folders. Those for which least training was reported were those which concern what happens to data after the end of a project: preparing datasets for long-term preservation; determining whether datasets ought to be preserved; preparing datasets for sharing with other researchers; and dealing with copyright, licensing, or IP issues. It also came as no real surprise to find that the two tasks researchers felt least confident about – dealing with copyright, licensing and IP issues and preparing datasets for long-term preservation – were also the areas in which they felt training would be most beneficial.
>
> DaMaRO, 2012

Developing research and researcher support services

While librarians have traditionally supported researchers in describing and applying metadata to their publications, an opportunity exists to extend their expertise to helping researchers at all points of the DCC curation lifecycle model. In light of the DaMaRO survey findings this section explores some of the emerging areas of librarian support for researchers in managing and curating their research data in the short and longer terms. The activities explored in this section are organized using those areas of activity identified by the DCC Curation Lifecycle model where librarians might play a new and active role as data intensive research becomes increasingly commonplace. The activities listed below include examples of practical activity drawn from ongoing work within the JISCMRD projects, JISC RDMTrain projects and the DCC's institutional engagements.

Conceptualize, create or receive: support for planning RDM

As noted earlier, many funding bodies now require researchers to submit a data management plan (DMP) at the proposal stage. DMPs should generally be about two to four pages long and cover practical aspects such as the data types, volume, formats and capture methods that will be used in the project. They should also make clear any ethical or intellectual property considerations that may affect data sharing and reuse in the short and longer term. Funders are keen to have evidence that data sharing has been considered and want some information about how and when data will be shared, along with some reference to longer-term preservation and accessibility. DMPs cannot be completed in isolation: they require input from multiple individuals across the institution. Librarians already serve as liaison points between other institutional support services and this experience will be invaluable when helping researchers to produce their DMPs, which should be viewed as living documents.

Providing guidance to researchers for licensing their data

The DaMaRO survey highlighted that licensing and assessing IPR are areas where researchers feel they need greater support. As funders increase their requirements for open access to both publications and underlying research data, the need for this support will continue to grow. Creative Common licences[15] are increasingly applied to publications and data but many researchers seemingly struggle with picking the right licence to meet their needs and in many cases choosing more restrictive licences than they need based on uncertainty (van Noorden, 2013). Getting licensing issues agreed at the outset of a project is essential and it is particularly important to clarify IPR in collaborative research endeavours before selecting any licence. As data reuse becomes more commonplace, researchers will also need to be sure that they understand others' data licences and are able to adhere to any restrictions on sharing and reuse in derived works.

Appraise and select

A key challenge for researchers is identifying what data they need to keep in order to adhere to publishers', funders' and institutional mandates. The DCC recommends that, as a minimum, anything that will be necessary for validating their published research findings should be retained. However, in many cases there may be additional data that researchers want to keep and there will also be a number of cases where researchers are legally bound to dispose of the data, depending on the conditions outlined in consent forms.

A model to help illustrate the various types of data that may be associated with the findings of a given research publication has been developed by the International Association of Scientific, Technical and Medical Publishers (STM) and the Opportunities for Data Exchange (ODE) (The Data Publication Pyramid, see Figure 5.2). All data, whether born digital, digitized or analogue need to be considered as part of any RDM plan. The model can be very helpful for librarians when working with researchers to determine exactly what research data outputs they have generated and identifying what must be kept to validate their research findings.

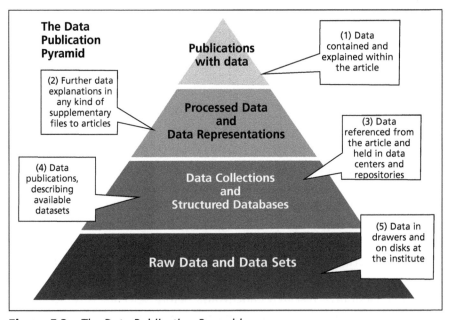

Figure 5.2 *The Data Publication Pyramid*
Reproduced with thanks from Reilly et al., 2011

It is important to remember that selection and appraisal decisions are happening from the earliest stage of new research, not just when researchers reach the end of their funded activity. Researchers are constantly making choices about capture tools, formats, compression, software and hardware – all of which might have implications for short- and longer-term access and reuse.

Case study: active selection at the University of Leeds

Selection and appraisal does not only happen at the point of ingest into a data repository. Selection and appraisal are taking place all the time in research activity. For instance, a researcher at the University of Leeds needs to scan spinal vertebrae images as part of his research. However, the researcher always chooses to capture a larger section of the spine than he needs to and at a higher resolution than is actually required. This is an active selection decision based on the fact that the most time-consuming and costly part of the imaging process lies in preparing the subject for imaging rather than the imaging process itself. By capturing more data than he needs, s/he is essentially expanding the amount of data available for future research at a fraction of the cost. The additional cost associated with a larger file size is outweighed by the potential savings to be made in carrying out future research and the potential value associated with reuse (RoaDMaP, 2013). ■

Access, use and reuse of research data

Reuse is a major benefit that may be realized from investing in managing and curating research data activity. Evidence supports the view that when researchers make their data accessible along with publications they can expect to see an increase in citations. However, researchers may need advice from librarians on how to make their data citable and what level of granularity they should use. Researchers may also need support in citing others' data (i.e. citing external data that has been used as part of new research activity).

In aiming to make citation as easy as possible for researchers, librarians might want to consider automating the generation of recommended citations once data has been deposited in a repository. For example, at the University of Exeter Data Archive (EDA) an automatically generated guide for citations is created once a dataset is ingested into the repository and the researcher receives notification via e-mail. The e-mail contains 'a permanent link to the work' and the e-mail urges researchers to 'cite this link in preference to the URL of the item as it provides continuing persistent access in case the URL should ever change' (University of Exeter EDA, n.d.). The EDA approach helps to ensure longer term accessibility to the data as well as making citation easier for reusers.

This short section illustrates just a few of the possible data curation lifecycle activities where librarians have the opportunity and the accompanying skills to add value to the process. The LIBER working group on E-Science/Research Data Management's *Ten Recommendations for Libraries to Get Started with Research Data Management* (Christensen-Dalsgaard et al., 2012) provides additional suggestions.

Building librarians' readiness to provide research data support
An assessment of librarians' RDM readiness

The leadership of the library in establishing and delivering institutional research data management infrastructure and support, as seen in a large number of the DCC's institutional engagements, demonstrates that there is recognition of the role and value of librarians' skills. There is also great potential for re-shaping the professional role of the librarian within the institution as these research data management support services mature and become increasingly vital to current and future research. However, to fully realize this vision, there are some areas where librarians may need to adapt and/or update their skills or acquire completely new skills. Research Libraries UK (RLUK) commissioned a study in 2012 (Auckland, 2012) which

---

The nine areas identified as having potentially the most significant skills gap are:

- Ability to advise on **preserving research outputs** (49% essential in 2–5 years; 10% now)
- Knowledge to advise on **data management and curation**, including ingest, discovery, access, dissemination, preservation and portability (48% essential in 2–5 years; 16% now)
- Knowledge to support researchers in **complying with the various mandates of funders**, including open access requirements (40% essential in 2–5 years; 16% now)
- Knowledge to advise on potential **data manipulation tools** used in the discipline/ subject (34% essential in 2–5 years; 7% now)
- Knowledge to advise on **data mining** (33% essential in 2–5 years; 3% now)
- Knowledge to advocate and advise on the use of **metadata** (29% essential in 2–5 years; 10% now)
- Ability to advise on the **preservation of project records**, e.g. correspondence (24% essential in 2–5 years; 3% now)
- Knowledge of **sources of research funding** to assist researchers to identify potential funders (21% essential in 2–5 years; 8% now)
- Skills to develop **metadata schema and advise on discipline/subject standards and practices**, for individual research projects (16% essential in 2–5 years; 2% now).

Figure 5.3 *Re-skilling for research*
Reproduced with thanks from Auckland, 2012

revealed nine key areas where librarians believe their skills gaps might be. Figure 5.3 on the previous page lists the nine areas identified in the study and outlines when librarians feel these skills will become essential for their effectiveness in their day to day activities.

Another recent survey, by Corrall, Kennan and Afzal, was undertaken to investigate current and planned services and support for research data management and bibliometrics across a number of international academic libraries. The findings indicate that:

> in many cases development of the types of specialized research support services investigated are constrained by knowledge and skills gaps among library staff and a lack of confidence surrounding their expected roles in both RDM and bibliometrics. While technical competencies in both bibliometrics and RDM scored highly among the areas where knowledge and skills were needed, our findings also demonstrate the importance of understanding the research environment at both macro and micro level for providing effective services for research. Corrall, Kennan and Afzal, 2013, 636

It would seem that while librarians have many of the core skills required for supporting some areas of research data management, it is clear that additional skills and increased confidence in some areas are considered necessary by many professionals in the field.

Bridging the librarians' skills gap

There has been an increase in the number of educational programmes covering aspects of data management and curation for emerging information science professionals in recent years. Sheila Corrall provides a very good summary of emerging educational programmes covering RDM for information science students in *Managing Research Data* (Pryor, 2012). There have also been some recent developments with regard to professional development opportunities for librarians already in the workplace. The following examples may be of particular interest for professional development.

DC101, tools of the trade and train the trainer materials

The DCC offers free courses that provide an introduction to research data management and curation. These introductory courses aim to give participants an understanding of the drivers and benefits for research data management and help staff engaged in support of research to identify practical ways to develop and sustain RDM support within their current institutional infrastructure. The DCC also offers half-day workshops on a range of DCC tools, including the Data Asset Framework (DAF) and DMP Online. These courses provide hands-on experience in applying the tools in an institutional setting. The DCC also provides access to a range of DC101 and JISC RDMTrain materials to help develop and deliver RDM training to staff within their own institutions.

3TU Data Intelligence 4 Librarians

The 3TU Federation is a consortium of the libraries of the Delft University of Technology, Eindhoven University of Technology and the University of Twente. The consortium provides a shared data service for researchers across the three institutions. In 2011, 3TU developed their Data Intelligence 4 Librarians course to help progress the 'professionalisation and positioning of the library and its employees to be a partner in the support of data-intensive science' (Data Intelligence 4 Librarians, 2012). The four-day course provides a mix of remote and face-to-face training and exercises designed to help librarians in post to develop and hone RDM skills. Topics include data citation, selection and legal issues.

RDMRose

RDMRose is 'a JISC funded project to produce taught and continuing professional development (CPD) learning materials in Research Data Management (RDM) tailored for Information professionals'.[16] The project is being run collaboratively by the libraries of the Universities of Leeds, Sheffield and York and will make use of the Information School at the University of Sheffield to disseminate the eight RDM modules, each of which equates to a half-day of study:

> One of the central assumptions made in the design of the module is that
> librarians themselves often do not have in-depth experience of research. RDM
> and an increasing number of other roles to support research require more
> understanding of the perspective of the researcher. Therefore considerable time
> in the module is devoted to actively exploring the nature of research and
> research data. The module also encourages you to think about the potential role

of other professional services, such as research administration and computing.

RDMRose, 2013

The modules are also being embedded into the postgraduate education for information professionals so that the skills of emerging and in-post librarians will be of a consistent quality.

The Digital Curator Vocational Education Europe (DigCurV) project

The DigCurV[17] project has been working to develop a vocational training framework for library, archives and museum staff. The project has also developed and maintains a registry of current international training opportunities that may be of value to librarians seeking to undertake professional development. The Library of Congress' Digital Preservation Outreach and Education (DPOE)[18] similarly provides access to a list of current training opportunities for different audiences from beginners to experts and runs a number of train the trainer workshops to improve librarians' skills (Library of Congress, 2012).

Conclusions

Francis Maude, UK Minister for the Cabinet Office and Paymaster General, refers to data as 'the 21st century's new raw material' (HM Government, 2012). Indeed, those who can claim to be data scientists are currently 'difficult and expensive to hire and, given the very competitive market for their services, difficult to retain' (Davenport and Patil, 2012). However, as dealing with data of all kinds, not just research data but administrative and financial data, is becoming increasingly ubiquitous in all walks of life, employers across all fields will be seeking recruits who have the ability to exploit and extract value from data. As noted by Hal Varian, Chief Economist at Google:

> The ability to take data – to be able to understand it, to process it, to extract value from it, to visualize it, to communicate it's going to be a hugely important skill in the next decades, not only at the professional level but even at the educational level for elementary school kids, for high school kids, for college kids.
>
> Varian, 2009

As Davenport says, 'think of big data as an epic wave gathering now, starting to crest. If you want to catch it, you need people who can surf' (Davenport and Patil, 2012). This changing landscape does pose a number of challenges for librarians as they carve out a niche in a world of data. However, librarians have risen to these sorts of challenges before and are well placed to capitalize on the new opportunities that are opening up. So, grab your surfboard, 'cause surf's up!'

Notes

1 www.dcc.ac.uk.
2 http://ec.europa.eu/research/index.cfm.
3 Nature Policy on Availability of data & materials, www.nature.com/authors/policies/availability.html.
4 http://figshare.com.
5 www.plos.org.
6 www.impactstory.org.
7 www.gigasciencejournal.com.
8 www.pangaea.de/about.
9 www.jisc.ac.uk/whatwedo/programmes/mrd.aspx.
10 http://as.exeter.ac.uk/library/resources/openaccess/openexeter/data.
11 www.dcc.ac.uk/resources/policy-and-legal/institutional-data-policies/uk-institutional-data-policies.
12 www.dcc.ac.uk/resources/policy-and-legal/institutional-roadmaps.
13 www.jisc.ac.uk/whatwedo/programmes/mrd/rdmtrain.aspx.
14 http://damaro.oucs.ox.ac.uk.
15 http://creativecommons.org.
16 http://rdmrose.blogspot.co.uk.
17 www.digcur-education.org/eng/Training-opportunities.
18 www.digitalpreservation.gov/education.

References

Auckland, M. (2012) *Re-skilling for Research: an investigation into the role and skills of subject and liaison librarians required to effectively support the evolving information needs of researchers*, RLUK, www.rluk.ac.uk/files/RLUK%20Re-skilling.pdf.

Christensen-Dalsgaard, B., Van den Berg, M., Grim, R., Horstmann, W., Jansen, D., Pollard, T. and Roos, A. (2012) Ten Recommendations for Libraries to Get Started with Research Data Management, Final report of the LIBER working group on E-Science/Research Data Management, www.libereurope.eu/sites/default/files/WGSC_20120801.pdf.

Corrall, S., Kennan, M. and Afzal W. (2013), Bibliometrics and Research Data Management Services: emerging trends in library support for research, *Library Trends*, **61** (3), 636–741.

DaMaRO (2012) *Research Data Management Training for the Sciences Survey*, http://blogs.ox.ac.uk/damaro/2013/01.

Data Intelligence 4 Librarians (2012) 3TU, http://dataintelligence.3tu.nl/en/home.

Davenport, T. H. and Patil, D. J. (2012) Data Scientist: the sexiest job of the 21st century, *Harvard Business Review*, **90** (10) 70–5.

Digital Curation Centre (n.d.) *What is digital curation?*, www.dcc.ac.uk/digital-curation.

Digital Science (2013) Press releases, www.digital-science.com/pages/press-releases#figshareforinstitutions.

Education for Change (2012) *Researchers of Tomorrow: the research behaviour of Generation Y doctoral students*, www.jisc.ac.uk/media/documents/publications/reports/2012/Researchers-of-Tomorrow.pdf.

EPSRC (2011) *Policy Framework on Research Data*, www.epsrc.ac.uk/about/standards/researchdata/Pages/default.aspx.

European Union (2010) *Riding the wave: how Europe can gain from the rising tide of scientific data*, http://cordis.europa.eu/fp7/ict/e-infrastructure/docs/hlg-sdi-report.pdf.

Guy, M., Donnelly, M. and Molloy, L. (2013) *Pinning It Down: towards a practical definition of 'research data' for creative arts institutions*, presented at 8th International Digital Curation Conference, Amsterdam, www.slideshare.net/MariekeGuy/pinning-it-down-towards-a-practical-definition-of-research-data-for-creative-arts-institutions?from_search=12.

Higgins, S. (2008) The DCC Curation Lifecycle Model, *International Journal of Digital Curation*, **3** (1), 134–40.

HM Government (2012) *Open Data White Paper: unleashing the potential*, http://data.gov.uk/sites/default/files/Open_data_White_Paper.pdf.

Jisc (2013) News release, www.jisc.ac.uk/news/international-digging-into-data-challenge-launches-05-feb-2013.

Knowledge Exchange (2011) *A Surfboard for Riding the Wave: towards a four country action programme on research data*, www.knowledge-exchange.info/surfboard.

Library of Congress (2012) *Digital Preservation Outreach and Education*, www.digitalpreservation.gov/education/index.html.

OECD (2007) *Principles and Guidelines for Access to Research Data from Public Funding*, www.oecd.org/science/scienceandtechnologypolicy/38500813.pdf.

Piwowar, H. A. (2013) Altmetrics: value all research products, *Nature*, **493**, 159.

Piwowar, H. A., Day, R. S. and Fridsma, D. B. (2007) Sharing Detailed Research Data is Associated with Increased Citation Rate, *PLoS ONE*, **2** (3), e308.

Pryor, G. (ed.) (2012) Managing Research Data, Facet Publishing, London.

RCUK (2010) *Common Principles on Data Policy*, www.rcuk.ac.uk/research/Pages/Datapolicy.aspx.

RCUK (2012) *Policy on Open Access to Research Outputs*, www.rcuk.ac.uk/research/Pages/outputs.aspx.

RDMRose (2013) http://rdmrose.group.shef.ac.uk.

Reilly, S., Schallier, W., Schrimpf, S., Smit, E. and Wilkinson, M. (2011) *Report on Integration of Data and Publications*, www.stm-assoc.org/2011_12_5_ODE_Report_On_Integration_of_Data_and_Publications.pdf.

RoaDMaP (2013) *RoaDMaP Project*, University of Leeds, http://library.leeds.ac.uk/roadmap-project.

University of Exeter Data Archive (n.d.) as.exeter.ac.uk/library/resources/openaccess/ore/.

University of Glasgow (2012) *Draft Research Data Policy*, www.gla.ac.uk/media/media_232425_en.docx.

van Noorden, R. (2013) Researchers Opt to Limit Uses of Open-access Publications, *Nature*, 6 February, www.nature.com/news/researchers-opt-to-limit-uses-of-open-access-publications-1.12384.

Varian, H. (2009) Hal Varian on How the Web Challenges Managers, *McKinsey Quarterly*, January, www.mckinseyquarterly.com/Hal_Varian_on_how_the_Web_challenges_managers.

CHAPTER 6

Learners and digital identity: the Digital Tattoo project

Julie Mitchell and Cindy Underhill

We all understand that an embarrassing photo could damage our reputation, but what are other, less obvious ways we might do so?

Teacher candidate, Faculty of Education, UBC.

My online networks all have very different values – friends, professional colleagues, family. Managing all of them gets complicated.

Undergraduate student, UBC.

Now that I'm graduating, I feel the pressure to build a brand. It's depressing.

Graduate student, UBC.

Introduction: our motivation

Students, like the rest of us, are leveraging the public (or quasi-public) nature of social media and related technologies to organize protests, collaborate on projects, document and share experiences, voice opinions, participate in like-minded communities, arrange social functions and share gossip. Though we have always used the media at hand to communicate with wider public circles than we typically interact with, the process usually took a bit of planning, organization and involved more than a single individual to make it happen. Today, anyone with a smartphone and an internet connection can post an image or video that can be viewed by hundreds or even millions, if public attention is captured. It is not uncommon for an aspiring musician to garner hundreds of views on a music video uploaded to YouTube, an art student to get hundreds of comments on an online exhibit created on Flickr or an aspiring journalist to get picked up by a major news source for a politically astute tweet or blog post. These are average people with individual access to a broad public audience via the free social media tools available today.

In a recent publication dedicated to themes related to socially mediated publicness, researchers Baym and Boyd (2012, 321) note that this 'level of moderate, widespread publicness is unprecedented' and brings with it both opportunities and challenges. The complexity of the multiple contexts and networks that students interact with, combined with technology that allows information to travel across contexts quickly and easily with the touch of a send button, requires both new literacies and new skills. Baym and Boyd (2012, 320) make the point that 'understanding socially-mediated publicness is an ever-shifting process throughout which people juggle blurred boundaries, multi-layered audiences, individual attributes, the specifics of the systems they use and the contexts of their use'. This is a process that takes time and, like any developmental process, involves mistakes. Mistakes that were once an expected and accepted part of the process of learning about good judgement that occurred mostly in private or close personal circles may now be made public and persistent as long as they remain published on the internet, either intentionally or inadvertently, depending on the user's understanding of the technology. Hargittai's (2008) research on skills among internet users has shown that people differ in how well prepared they are to manage these processes and make wise choices.

Real choice requires sufficient information, skill, self-awareness and time for learning about how to leverage the technology that is available so that we can participate and contribute and yet preserve and protect the aspects of ourselves that we want to keep private. Approaches for supporting the development of these capacities are still emerging, but promising on this front are Howard Rheingold's five literacies for thriving online, which include attention, crap detection, participation, collaboration and network smarts (Rheingold, 2012, 246–51). These literacies are about behaviours that can support sound decision-making when it comes to digital participation.

At the University of British Columbia, librarians recognized that professional staff had a role in supporting the development of digital literacy as students were grappling with the impact of their online participation on the formation of their digital identities. The blurring of lines between identities as student, emerging professional and private individual meant that professional staff needed to be equipped to mentor and support students as they struggled to develop the skills they needed. Indeed, according to the 2012 Horizon Report '[d]igital media literacy continues its rise in importance as a key skill in every discipline and profession' (Johnson, Adams and Cummins, 2012, 6). But what exactly are those skills? What format would best suit the fast-paced and ever-evolving landscape of the themes and issues related to digital identity, reputation and social media? Where were we going to start?

The following chapter describes the Digital Tattoo project at the University of British Columbia and its focus on supporting learners to make informed choices and extend their digital capabilities around online practices, safety and identity. We will provide background on this innovative project and describe the multi-professional team structure that drives the project forward. We will discuss benefits, challenges and what we have learned in creating and sustaining this dynamic, flexible learning resource. Finally, we will address project outcomes and future directions, including highlights from a recent study conducted by the Digital Tattoo project team pertaining to student perceptions of social media and digital identity. Stretching the boundaries of traditional librarianship, the project emphasizes the role of partnership between learners, librarians and professional staff in creating an environment for ongoing innovation in an ever-changing digital landscape.

Our project
What we set out to do

The goal of the Digital Tattoo project is to provide support for students to develop responsible, judicious and analytical approaches to their decisions regarding their online identities: specifically, what to share, with whom and how best to participate across varied networks, both as a consumer and as a creator. Comprising a website, workshop curriculum and teaching resources, the project aims to raise questions, provide examples and highlight resources to encourage learners to think about their presence online; help navigate the issues involved in shaping their digital identity; and educate learners about their rights and responsibilities as digital citizens. The idea for the Digital Tattoo project was conceived in 2007, after librarians at UBC recognized the need to support students around issues of digital identity. The library looked for partners to develop a proposal for a project and in 2008, those partners formed an advisory committee that drove the initial development. The advisory committee secured project funding through UBC's Teaching and Learning Enhancement Fund and hired the first group of students to work on the project.

Underpinning the Digital Tattoo project are notions of participatory culture and digital literacy that come from the work of media scholar Henry Jenkins (Jenkins, 2009) and critic, writer and teacher Howard Rheingold (Rheingold, 2012). Specifically, both of these experts highlight the importance of social competency, understanding networks and how they operate and negotiating across varied contexts with different people, who have different values, expectations and spoken (or more often, unspoken) rules of conduct. This is much more complex than just learning how to use or manage a particular tool or technology. It requires a level of self-awareness and reflection that takes time, maturity and experience to develop. As explained by Jenkins:

> Most public policy discussion of new media has centred on technologies – tools and their affordances. . . . Our goals should be to encourage youth to develop the skills, knowledge, ethical frameworks and self-confidence needed to be full participants in contemporary culture.   Jenkins, 2009, 6–7

While an emphasis on developing knowledge and encouraging personal reflection is central to the Digital Tattoo project, professional staff hear from students that they want practical information and something they can easily act on. As stated by Rheingold (2012, 8), however, '[t]here is no single recipe for a mindful life in the digital mediasphere; reflection is required'. In order to balance the need for both reflection and practical guidance, the Digital Tattoo website themes, workshop curriculum and teaching resources introduce questions for reflection and discussion while also offering opportunities to take action that encourage the user to go deeper into these subtle and critically important understandings and address their practical concerns related to their own use of digital tools and social media. Covering issues such as cyberbullying, geotagging, collaborative online learning, copyright and digital identity as it impacts career prospects, the topics are varied and wide-ranging.

The concept of digital permanence was particularly motivating for the project. The notion that once you publish something online it is difficult, if not impossible, to remove (much like a tattoo) resonated with the student team members. And, like a tattoo, your digital identity is personal, even though it is shaped in part by what others say about you. A broad goal of the project was to make sure that visitors to the site were provided with the information and resources that would help them develop the awareness and foundational skills to make wise decisions that would support the kind of 'digital tattoo' they wanted to create and build for themselves. The tattoo metaphor prevailed and became the title for the project: digitaltattoo.ubc.ca.

How we did it
Gather the right people and expertise

Digital Tattoo advisory committee members included project students plus representatives from UBC Library, the Centre for Teaching, Learning and Technology, Student Development, Career Services, Access and Diversity Services and the Writing Centre. This group met early on to establish a direction for a website and workshop curriculum around five basic themes: social networking, protecting privacy, employment, new opportunities for learning and publishing and research. The multi-professional nature of the advisory committee brought different perspectives and unique expertise that were invaluable to the ongoing development of the Digital Tattoo project. At the same time, the fact that members of this team came from diverse perspectives, and had varying levels of engagement with issues around digital identity, made it important to establish principles that the group could agree on and would guide decision-making. These guiding principles include:

- Currency and relevance of content is critical.
- Students are in the best position to identify relevant content themes.
- There is no single 'right way' to be online. Identity is individual. However, wise choices require informed individuals.
- Well researched information provides guidance for wise decision-making.
- Consistency, simplicity and opportunities for deeper investigation allow for optimum user experience.

Development of these guiding principles was critical for decision-making about content, approach to workshop delivery and web design. These guidelines remain central to the work of the project team today and support the annual orientation of new project students.

While the advisory committee set strategic directions for the project, development, delivery and ongoing maintenance of resources requires the expertise of a smaller multi-professional project team and leadership from student-staff. The project team implementing this initiative currently consists of three students (both graduate and undergraduate), a Learning Resource Design Strategist (with expertise in learning design and online resource development), a librarian and members of the technical team from UBC's Centre for Teaching, Learning and Technology. This group provides a foundation of expertise (both technical and pedagogical) which is necessary for mentorship, guidance and support for students as they develop their research, writing, networking, technical and facilitation skills.

Assemble the right strategies and tools

To support the guiding principles established by the advisory committee, the project working team identified several practical strategies to guide website development and curriculum creation. These strategies include the following:

- student-generated content to ensure relevance
- simple, reusable learning design to maximize flexibility and facilitate reflection, understanding and action
- re-publishing strategies (such as RSS, embed, etc.) to allow for publishing in multiple contexts and keep content current
- Creative Commons licence to support flexible reuse
- use of social media to engage conversation
- WordPress platform to support timely editing/publishing
- blogging as response to current issues (i.e. news)
- accessible teaching resources (hosted in Slideshare, UBCwiki and YouTube) to support community-based discussion and workshops.

Given that numerous authors are involved in creating and delivering content, it is essential that the platforms used to host the Digital Tattoo project resources support collaboration. The platforms, which include UBC hosted WordPress and MediaWiki installations and a project management tool called Active Collab, are relatively easy to learn and are part of the University's technical infrastructure, ensuring that training and support are well integrated. This contributes to the sustainability of the project by allowing for short training timelines and ongoing technical support for new student team members. The Digital Tattoo team also makes use of the social web to host our resources (YouTube and Slideshare) and to facilitate discussion or comment on themes that students are blogging about via Facebook and Twitter.

Engage with the community

Digital Tattoo workshops are delivered throughout the year both face-to-face and online, related to the themes addressed on the website. Workshops are designed to encourage discussion and exploration of themes around digital identity in a more social environment. Workshop requests may come from the UBC community or from schools or public libraries province-wide. To foster long-term sustainability of the project, a train-the-trainer model is in place whereby workshops, lessons plans and teaching resources are available online for others to download. Digital Tattoo project leads will often go into the community to deliver a workshop or run a discussion group on a theme related to digital identity, with the agreement that a delegate at the host library or institution attends the workshop to learn to deliver future sessions in that community using Digital Tattoo resources and adapting them to local needs.

The Digital Tattoo project has now been in place for five years and it continues to be a popular resource. With consistent annual web traffic of over 20,000 visitors and continued requests for workshops both locally and nationally, the website and workshop curriculum have proved to be an important resource for the campus and greater community. By bringing together a diverse, multi-professional advisory committee, developing a clear project framework, honouring a student-led approach and utilizing tools to facilitate collaboration among the project team, the Digital Tattoo project pooled campus expertise on digital identity to create a resource to extend learners' digital capabilities.

What we learned
Mentor students and let them lead

A unique feature of the Digital Tattoo project is the emphasis on student-generated content. Identified by the advisory committee at the outset of the project as a key guiding principle, the direction students provide with respect to content development helps us to stay current and fluid in the development of our resources. Students conduct and post video interviews; maintain and update the website; write relevant and timely blog posts; manage the Digital Tattoo social media strategy; and deliver workshops. These activities require students to learn independently, take risks, stay flexible and rely on each other for feedback and support. First attempts at some of these activities, which may be new to some of our students, may not always be successful. We work at creating a learning environment, where failure is expected, success is celebrated and learning from each other is encouraged.

Project students are supported by the expertise and mentorship provided by the professional staff on the working team. Mentorship may include joint examination of resources, discussion of responsibilities as a content creator, review of content dealing with legal or sensitive issues, attribution for embedded content and understanding copyright. Broadly, students are informally mentored in the development of skills related to learning design, research, information management and digital literacy. However, it is the personal knowledge and experience that project students bring, regarding how they and their peers understand and learn about their digital tattoos, that is central to the success of the project. In creating and delivering workshops, for example, student team members have been successful in drawing out new ideas from their peers which have informed successful strategies for engaging groups of students. In addition, students and staff connect with their networks, asking for feedback on the website and leveraging those networks to promote workshops and Digital Tattoo resources to their peers. They are experimenting, reflecting, generating feedback and applying new ideas to future experiences – exactly the kind of experiential learning and iterative design process we strive for in our work.

Clearly, the student-directed approach results in more relevant content for the website and workshops, but there are other benefits. As students are researching and talking about issues related to digital identity, they are learning a great deal about their own digital identity. As noted by project team student Paul Chiang, undergraduate student in the Faculty of Arts at UBC,

Working on the Digital Tattoo project has definitely instilled in me a certain kind of cautiousness when I, say, view and post things on my Facebook profile. Not surprising when most of the top stories circulating the internet regarding digital identity are about how people have, using social media, carelessly ruined their own lives. But horror stories aside, I am also beginning to realize just how powerful social media technology can be, when properly applied, in empowering not just the user, but whole groups of people with a common goal, either on a community level, a national level, or even on a global level.

E-mail message to author, 2013

Professional staff observe the transformational learning that occurs with project students with respect to digital identity as they work on the website, develop reflection activities and deliver workshops.

While maintaining a student-directed approach is a fundamental value of the Digital Tattoo project, it is not without its challenges. Internships, study abroad opportunities and competing demands on student time mean that trained student-staff may only stay on the team for an academic year or may leave the position midway through the academic term, leaving the professional staff to re-hire and re-train frequently. With the student-directed approach to this project and a small team, such transitions can be quite disruptive to workflow, website content management and workshop commitments. Another challenge relates to support and mentorship of project students. To do this well requires professional staff to be skilled at identifying areas of strength and need on the project working team, each time there is a change in members. Depending on the strengths or gaps on the project team at any one time, we may need to shift the focus temporarily while we work together to ensure that each student develops the competencies they need to fulfil their role.

While student appointments come to the position with a strong knowledge of social web tools and approaches, it is an ongoing challenge to equip the student team members with the expertise they require around Creative Commons licensing and Canadian copyright guidelines in order to work on the website and update teaching resources. While a strong suite of orientation resources exists for new project students, these require regular updating due to the ebbs and flows around current policy and practice (particularly related to copyright), version updates to technical platforms used to support the project and strategies adopted by the University to meet the demand for mobile-friendly websites and resources. As evident from the range of changes listed, we would not be effective in addressing these without the range of expertise and experience that a multi-professional team provides.

Collaboration is a commitment

The challenges that exist in working with the student team are not only balanced by the benefits of working with students, but also with the benefits of a multi-professional team environment. In addition to the student team, the Digital Tattoo project involves one Learning Resource Design Strategist and one librarian in the professional staff member complement. These two skill sets work particularly well for the Digital Tattoo project, as they bring different perspectives around learning design, technology, content organization, teaching and workshop delivery, student-staff supervision and information architecture. Specifically, the Learning Resource Design Strategist was instrumental in developing the learning design framework for the project, creating design templates and developing key questions to support the students' work to create the content modules and workshop curriculum and acting as a 'technical translator' between the applications support team and the project team. The librarian was invaluable in contributing expertise related to information architecture, copyright, attribution and student-staff administration. Not only do these different professional perspectives and expertise benefit the project, they also benefit the professional staff members involved, who have the opportunity to learn from each other as each person brings awareness of issues from different professional spheres. In more traditional roles, librarians may not have the opportunity to work with a Learning Resource Design Strategist – however, management of the Digital Tattoo project involves ongoing collaboration between the two professionals, who co-lead the work. Through this collaboration, the librarian is exposed to literature, theories, ideas and concepts outside his or her discipline, broadening expertise and expanding knowledge beyond the library realm. Notably, as the project has progressed and professional staff learn from each other, the demarcation of roles and traditional boundaries lessen. The focus shifts away from the specific expertise that each professional contributes to the project to an emphasis on the knowledge, skills and resources that need to be developed by each team member for the project to be successful.

The benefits observed with respect to librarian involvement in this project reinforce Shumaker's (2012) work on embedded librarianship. As noted by Shumaker, as the librarian's engagement with the team progresses,

> the embedded librarian develops highly customized, sophisticated and value-added contributions to the team – contributions that sometimes go far beyond the confines of traditional reference work and that some might be surprised to find a librarian delivering.   Shumaker, 2012, 23

In any given day, the librarian project co-lead for Digital Tattoo may be asked to give a radio interview about digital literacy, respond to a workshop participant who is worried about a 'racy' video on YouTube or mentor a student-staff member to compose blog posts on digital identity from a balanced perspective. Contrary to a more traditional model where a librarian may wait at the reference desk to be asked questions, the librarian for this project is an active member of a multi-professional team, developing specialized skills and knowledge around digital identity.

There is a wealth of examples in the literature that highlight librarians and information professionals working on multi-professional teams, particularly with respect to medical librarianship (i.e. Tan and Maggio, 2013; Lorenzetti and Rutherford, 2012; Kenefick, 2011; Schwing and Coldsmith, 2005). There is also much written on the benefits of embedded librarianship, where librarians move outside the confines of the library to join a specialized research group or locate services within a particular faculty or department (i.e. Schulte, 2012; Kvenild and Calkins, 2011; Drewes and Hoffman, 2010; Freiburger and Kramer, 2009). In the case of the Digital Tattoo project, however, a librarian did not simply join an existing group, she initiated the project and brought a multi-professional team together to support student needs around digital literacy. Such initiatives demonstrate a shift in librarianship from that of service to the institution to a leadership role within the campus community in identifying student need and initiating solutions.

While the benefits of a multi-professional team environment are an unquestionable asset to the project, there are also challenges encountered that present opportunities for growth. With different professional perspectives may come differences of opinion on how to proceed with the project. Co-supervision of the student team may also present challenges if supervision styles differ between project co-leads. For both issues, clearly communicating expectations, honouring the needs of the project and trusting in each other's abilities is essential. With regard to co-supervision, being open to differences of opinion and approaches between professional staff and working through them respectfully and visibly with students allow the project to proceed in a timely manner, while role-modelling, for the student team, professional strategies which help negotiate differences of opinion.

Finally, while collaboration is a key to the success of the project, there is also a cost in terms of staff time that may be invisible from a budgetary perspective. Specifically, working through differences and moving forward collaboratively simply takes more time than moving forward on a project independently. And when strategic priorities may differ between departments of a multi-professional team a secondary layer of complexity is added. With this challenge, it is important to be transparent to senior management regarding the 'cost' of collaboration in terms of time and accurately assigning the time commitment required on a project. Often, senior management may believe that dividing a project among departments cuts the work in half – in reality, however, the collaborative element takes time and needs to be budgeted for accordingly.

Sustainable practices are essential

Aside from the student-led approach and multi-professional work environment, a unique benefit and challenge of the Digital Tattoo project relates to the content itself. The issue of digital identity stretches across multiple fields of expertise and evolves at a rate that can make it difficult to stay well informed. Developing the expertise to create and deliver workshops on this content and mentor students on updating project resources stretches the boundaries of traditional librarianship, which may focus more on reference, collection development and subject liaison responsibilities. At the same time, it engages skills inherent in more traditional roles such as current awareness strategies, research expertise, copyright knowledge, information architecture and teaching and workshop delivery. In applying these skills, knowledge around digital identity develops through ongoing engagement with the content.

A challenge with the project overall – one familiar in the library profession – is information management and organization of content. Whether it is maintaining current web content, updating and organizing teaching resources or developing training materials for students, the rapid rate at which content evolves, combined with the vast amount of content on the topic, is an ongoing challenge for the Digital Tattoo project team. A strategy to overcome this challenge includes clearly defining the project scope, constant assessment and weeding of web content and a sustainable content maintenance schedule that accounts for the inherent turnover in the student-staff team.

A final challenge with the project is simply maintaining balance when only a small portion of each professional team member's time is assigned to the project. The size and scope of the project could easily demand full-time commitment from two professional staff – however, as with many projects, there is not the luxury to devote such time. With approximately 20% of each staff member's time available to devote to the Digital Tattoo project, a constant eye to sustainability is required. Examples of this were referred to earlier with strategies like a content management system that can easily be learned by new student-staff, self-directed learning resources for new student team members and a strategy of hiring student-staff who can work well independently with little supervision.

Making a difference

Analysis of Digital Tattoo website analytics shows that although the majority of our visitors are from North America, our site is accessed by people as far away as Australia, India and the Philippines. We have consistent traffic on the site of more than 20,000 visitors annually, more than 4000 people accessing the teaching resources on our wiki and over 12,000 users accessing our various videos on YouTube. From such statistics, we know that people are using our resources, but are they having an impact? We recently explored this question in our work with UBC's Teacher Education Program.

Over the past three years, project leads have delivered workshops to all incoming teacher candidates, typically over 500 students each year. Recently, project co-leads collaborated with a faculty member in Education to design and deliver an online survey to measure the practices of teacher candidates as it relates to their use of social media and the impact of the Digital Tattoo workshops on their attitudes. In September 2012, a short pre-survey was delivered to teacher candidate students prior to a Digital Tattoo workshop and a post-survey was delivered directly after the workshop. The pre-survey consisted of 11 closed-ended questions (yes/no and multiple choice) and one open-ended question. The post-survey consisted of eight closed-ended questions (multiple choice) and two open-ended questions. A total of 344 students responded to the pre-survey, 276 responded to the post-survey and a positive shift in student perceptions around social media was documented. For example, for the statement 'Teachers have a role in teaching students about the use of social media', 87% of students agreed with the statement on the pre-survey, compared with 91% on the post-survey, an increase of 4%. Similarly, for the statement 'Teachers have a role in shaping social media policy for the profession', 84% of students agreed with this statement on the pre-survey, compared with 90% on the post-survey, an increase of 6%. Finally, for the statement 'It's my responsibility as a teacher to decide how to use social media with my students', 76% of students agreed with this statement on the pre-survey compared with 82% on the post-survey, another increase of 6%. Overall, results point to the success of the workshops in shifting student perceptions around digital identity.

Such assessment and reporting out around the impact of the Digital Tattoo project on student learning is particularly critical, as the budget for the project is uncertain moving forward. Being able to clearly articulate the value of this project for the library, the University and the students it serves is more important than ever before. At the time the project was conceived, there was a dearth of practical resources around digital identity. Today, there are countless online resources available to a broad range of audiences: youth, teachers and parents. How can the Digital Tattoo project remain relevant and current given the changes in the digital landscape? What unique value do the site and workshops provide that other resources do not? In order to secure ongoing funding, project leads will need to answer these questions and continue to demonstrate the impact of the work on students' attitudes to their digital identities.

Looking ahead

A future challenge for the Digital Tattoo project is the tension between our goals in relation to digital literacy and critical thinking and what students often say they want – sensational stories about digital reputation gone wrong and step-by-step instructions for avoiding damage to their own. For example, in the author's survey of UBC teacher candidates, 93% of those who participated in our workshop agreed that the content would improve their abilities to manage their online identities, yet many wanted step-by-step advice and 'more scary stories' to illustrate the consequences of missteps and misunderstandings of the impact of networks. This finding is consistent with the literature on novice-expert skill development (Bransford, 2000; Dreyfus, 2004). Novices typically rely on rules, guidelines and facts in attending to problems or new learning situations. Experts act almost intuitively, drawing on deep and connected knowledge structures and experiences. In terms of digital identity, perhaps we are all somewhere in between novice and expert, because of the shifting landscape and complex technical, legal and privacy issues that arise. In this space between, we learn to recognize patterns and principles, associate new learning with what we already know and practice solving increasingly complex problems. With the Digital Tattoo Project, we help students build competency and expertise when we work to associate their own experiences and prior knowledge with new learning, correcting misconceptions along the way. Opportunities to dig deep into their own and others' stories (scary and hopeful), while uncovering the underlying principles at play, helps to lay the groundwork for developing competence and expertise. Tips and strategies are useful, but not sufficient if our goal is to encourage students to make thoughtful and informed decisions about their own digital identities.

This speaks to the importance of the emotional hooks for students who are viewing our site: that is, that they want to recognize themselves in the content. How do we raise provocative questions that stimulate interest and encourage personal reflection? How might we effectively use the media-generated 'worst-case scenarios' that some students find instructive as a springboard for critical analysis and discussion related to potential impact on digital identity?

Maintaining a balanced approach in writing about these issues is also an ongoing challenge for project students who work on the Digital Tattoo website. We need to continue to think carefully about how best to support our project students who are authoring this content, since this kind of work requires a sophisticated understanding and synthesis of the goals we are trying to achieve. One strategy could be the use of a set of literacies to provide project students with a better framework for developing questions and content. As mentioned in the introduction, Howard Rheingold's five literacies for thriving online (attention, crap detection, participation, collaboration and network smarts) are straightforward and the practical considerations he articulates for each literacy could provide a preliminary framework for our project students in the development of reflection questions related to our current content themes (Rheingold, 2012, 246).

As we continually look at improving our content themes, an ongoing consideration is current perceptions of students around their digital identities. While today's students clearly understand the impact of a misplaced photo, video or comment, they appear less savvy about how to create and manage an online identity to promote themselves via e-portfolio, blog or professional networking site. In our survey of teacher candidates at UBC, for example, only 33% used social media (LinkedIn or Facebook) for professional networking. The project team is also aware that students are looking for simple, immediate solutions to challenges faced by social media and may not want to take the time to build or reshape the digital identity they aspire to. It is a challenge familiar to librarians who offer information literacy instruction where new students want research to be simple, easy and instantaneous – although we know that is not always the case, even with the best tools on hand. Similarly, the Digital Tattoo project teams find that students want to 'push the easy button' when it comes to managing their digital identities. Students have reported to us that managing their online identities and contributing to others' identities (i.e. via online recommendations for friends and colleagues) is 'too much work' so they opt out of various communities or fall back to communication technologies that they understand to be more private in nature (i.e. text messaging) and therefore less work to maintain. These attitudes may reflect a relationship with technology that is more about fear of public scrutiny than community building or contributions to a collective. They may also reflect a lack of commitment to digital identity as something important and worthy of time and energy.

Students are just beginning to come to terms with the notion that it is important to cope with material on the internet that we may be embarrassed about. One way to achieve this is to create new content that reflects our current selves and write our own stories instead of falling victim to internet history. This approach takes time and thoughtful decision-making, which runs counter to student expectations of immediacy – shaped by hours of participation on mobile communication platforms and social media. How do we inspire students to invest the time it takes to move beyond instant gratification to thoughtful participation? How can we leverage the Digital Tattoo project to build a stronger online community so that students can share stories and resources with each other? Answering these questions goes beyond the Digital Tattoo project and relates to challenges in reimagining the learning environment at universities as a whole.

Conclusion: ongoing engagement

In his book *Net Smart: how to thrive online*, Rheingold (2012, 3) makes the point that 'digital literacies can make the difference between being empowered or manipulated, serene or frenetic'. Involvement in today's participatory culture requires a set of core skills and cultural competencies that range from experimentation, navigation across contexts and sound judgement to a sophisticated understanding of networks and how to negotiate across diverse communities, respecting multiple perspectives and synthesizing and making sense of complex interactions (Jenkins, 2009). This kind of learning is best supported when integrated thoughtfully into the fabric of a student's life: at home with family, in formal courses, experimenting and socializing with friends and in pursuing professional and amateur interests.

If we accept Jenkins' suggestion that literacy in the 21st century should be seen as social skills and competencies preparing us for contribution in diverse public spaces rather than simply personal expression or promotion of ourselves as 'brands', then we need to examine what this means in the context of our classrooms, curriculum and learning activities and ensure that we articulate this in a way that shows students that it matters. In a time when academic libraries are reinventing themselves, librarians in particular need to look at how they can play a role in helping students develop these digital literacy skills. As indicated in the 2012 Horizon Report '[d]espite the widespread agreement on the importance of digital media literacy, training in the supporting skills and techniques is rare in teacher education and non-existent in the preparation of most university faculty' (Johnson, Adams and Cummins, 2012, 6). At the University of British Columbia, students, librarians and professional staff are taking the lead on this front through the Digital Tattoo project, working collaboratively to help students develop the skills they require to face today's rich and complex digital environment.

References

Baym, N. K. and Boyd, D. (2012) Socially Mediated Publicness: an introduction, *Journal of Broadcasting & Electronic Media*, **56** (3), 320–29.

Bransford, J. (2000) *How People Learn: brain, mind, experience and school*, National Academy Press, Washington DC.

Drewes, K. and Hoffman, N. (2010) Academic Embedded Librarianship: an introduction, *Public Services Quarterly*, **6** (2), 75–82.

Dreyfus, S. E. (2004) The Five-Stage Model of Adult Skill Acquisition, *Bulletin of Science, Technology & Society*, **24** (3), 177–81.

Freiburger, G. and Kramer, S. (2009) Embedded Librarians: one library's model for decentralized service, *Journal of the Medical Library Association*, **97** (2), 139–42.

Hargittai, E. (2008) The Role of Expertise in Navigating Links of Influence. In Turow, J. and Tsui, L. (eds), *The Hyperlinked Society*, University of Michigan Press, Michigan.

Jenkins, H. (2009) *Confronting the Challenges of Participatory Culture: media education for the 21st century*, MIT Press, Cambridge, MA.

Johnson, L., Adams, S. and Cummins, M. (2012) *The NMC Horizon Report: 2012 higher education edition*, The New Media Consortium, Austin, Texas.

Kenefick, C. (2011) The Case for Embedded Hospital Librarianship, *Journal of Hospital Librarianship*, **11** (2), 195–9.

Kvenild, C. and Calkins, K. (2011) *Embedded Librarians: moving beyond one-shot instruction*, Association of College and Research Libraries, Chicago, IL.

Lorenzetti, D. L. and Rutherford, G. (2012) Information Professionals' Participation in Interdisciplinary Research: a preliminary study of factors affecting successful collaborations, *Health Information & Libraries Journal*, **29** (4), 274–84.

Rheingold, H. (2012) *Net Smart: how to thrive online*, MIT Press, Cambridge, MA.

Schulte, S. J. (2012) Embedded Academic Librarianship: a review of the literature, *Evidence Based Library and Information Practice*, **7** (4), 122–38.

Schwing, L. J. and Coldsmith, E. E. (2005) Librarians as Hidden Gems in a Clinical

Team, *Medical Reference Services Quarterly*, **24** (1), 29–39.

Shumaker, D. (2012) *The Embedded Librarian: innovative strategies for taking knowledge where it's needed*, Information Today, Inc., Medford, NJ.

Tan, M. C. and Maggio, L. A. (2013) Expert Searcher, Teacher, Content Manager and Patient Advocate: an exploratory study of clinical librarian roles, *Journal of the Medical Library Association*, **101** (1), 63.

THEME 3

Rethinking resource delivery

CHAPTER 7

Mobilizing your library

Kay Munro, Karen Stevenson,
Rosemary Stenson and Wendy Walker

Introduction

Keeping the library relevant in an increasingly digital world presents challenges for the effective management and delivery of library services. While there are many opportunities for libraries to operate in this environment, ensuring that library services meet stakeholder needs and expectations may be best served by taking a strategic approach to service development. This chapter focuses on the role of strategy in the digital environment, using the development and implementation of a mobile strategy at the University of Glasgow library as a case study.

Context

Until relatively recently, access to the internet was dependent on having a desktop or laptop computer. However, today a growing number of people are likely to access digital content across a multitude of mobile devices. Increasing sales of smartphones and tablets, the flexibility of web content and the introduction of 4G networks are creating consumers who expect on-the-go access to the internet whenever they want it. In the UK, nearly one-third of page views are now from smartphones (24%) and tablets (6.8%) and this trend is growing monthly (comScore, 2013). According to a report from mobile manufacturer Ericsson,[1] by 2015 80% of people accessing the internet will be doing so from mobile devices.

In the higher education sector, surveys of UK universities reflect a similar growth in web activity on mobile devices, with statistics showing visits to university websites from mobile browsers increasing by as much as 200%

from November 2010 to November 2011 (Power, 2012). The Horizon report on the technology outlook for UK tertiary education speculates that the next generation of students will be owners of internet-capable mobile devices that they will want to use for learning (Johnson and Adams, 2011).

Background

Staff at the University of Glasgow library took an early interest in mobile developments and a Mobile Technologies Group (MTG) was formed during 2010. In common with many libraries, the original focus was primarily on the development of a mobile interface for catalogue search and library account functionality. Investigation into the potential use of SMS (short message service) for circulation notices and instant messaging for reference and enquiry services was also explored. However two factors prompted a re-assessment of the range and scope of this project. Data from Google Analytics showed that although mobile traffic was small in relation to desktop browser access, it was steadily growing. This coincided with an increasing body of evidence in the professional literature about the current status of mobile services in libraries and predictions for the future. It was clear that there was an opportunity to think more widely about the introduction of mobile services. The library's senior management team recommended that the group take a more strategic approach to the implementation of mobile services than had originally been envisaged.

Creating strategy

The MTG began by looking for evidence of good practice in strategy development. The *JISC Strategy InfoKit* (Jisc, 2010) sets out what are believed to be 'the most important tasks and processes required to successfully articulate, co-ordinate and manage strategic activity' and defines certain key stages in strategy development and implementation. This particular version is no longer available on the Jisc website and has been replaced by a series of separate InfoKits; the most useful for the group's purposes were 'Defining and Articulating your Vision, Mission and Values' and 'Managing Strategic Activity'.[2]

A vital element identified in the InfoKit is that those responsible for strategic planning and activity have 'all relevant facts at their disposal' (Jisc, 2010). At Glasgow, a systematic review of the academic literature was undertaken and a decision was made to survey the library users and ask them what library services they would like to be able to access on their mobile devices. Showers (2012) reminds us that 'the user is at the heart of mobile transformation' and, as mobile embeds itself into the expectations of our everyday lives, understanding user expectations will be vital to future service planning.

Engagement with colleagues in other departments at the University was also explored. However, at that time, there was very little evidence of mobile development taking place at the University and no overall institutional strategy for mobile, and so a decision was made to develop a library-specific strategy. This situation was not unusual in the UK, as a 2010 Jisc review of mobile and wireless technologies confirmed, noting that libraries had 'led the way when it comes to pragmatic, learner-focused use of mobile technologies' (Belshaw, 2010). A recent review of the literature would suggest that the UK experience is not unique. A report of an Executive Roundtable on Mobile Devices and Platforms for the Coalition for Networked Information (2012) indicated that in North America only a minority of institutions had an overall institutional strategy for mobile and that in many cases, individual units, programmes or schools have begun to engage with mobile where they had a particular sense of urgency related to their programme or service that preceded readiness by the institution as a whole.

The strategy paper produced at Glasgow was a composite document that contained the following elements:

- vision for mobile
- ten high-level aims across a wide range of services
- strategic work plan for the first phase of activity.

The first vision for mobile had devices at the centre: 'to keep the library at the leading edge of new and emerging trends in mobile communication, we must deliver services that support the new generation of mobile devices and associated user expectations'. This would be revised in the second phase, when the emphasis shifted from the devices to the user and their expectations: 'to transform access to information in innovative ways that will engage and empower our users through the powerful features that modern mobile devices offer'.

The ten areas of strategic priority highlighted in the strategy document can be grouped into major themes:

- annual mobile survey of library users
- development of a mobile website incorporating catalogue search
- infrastructural elements, including Wi-Fi, Bluetooth, QR codes
- reference and enquiry services, including instant messaging, SMS and roving
- digital media skills for both library staff and library users
- communication – marketing to key stakeholders and users
- Live Lab – devices, testing and exploration.

The individual work plans created for each area of activity included a set of targets which could be achieved during the first phase. In some cases these were investigative, while others related to service development. Where possible, an identification of potential barriers was included.

The original mobile strategy paper, including the work plan, was endorsed by both the library senior management team and the library committee. The library committee is a University-level committee, chaired by a member of the University of Glasgow management group, with academic representatives from each of the four colleges. Management endorsement of any strategy is vital. At Glasgow, the MTG reports to the library's service development committee, which is convened by the Assistant Director with responsibility in this area. This ensures that the aims of the mobile strategy are communicated at a higher level and aligned with the overall library strategic plan.

Co-ordinating strategic activity

Strategic activities are co-ordinated by the MTG to ensure that planning is consistent with high-level objectives. Planning for mobile must also be flexible enough to allow for constant review and change in response to the rapidly changing technological landscape and stakeholder needs and expectations. At Glasgow, a cyclical approach to strategy implementation has been adopted, each cycle spanning one academic year. Since 2010 there have been three phases of strategic activity.

Strategic planning typically begins in the summer vacation. The MTG reviews all the activity of the previous phase, including analysis of the annual mobile surveys that provide the user perspective. A review of the academic and technical literature on developments in mobile since the previous planning phase is also undertaken. All of this information allows for an evaluation of the impact across the strategy as a whole and for priorities for the next phase of strategic activity to be set.

When priorities for the annual work plan are agreed, specific targets are then set. Targets are assigned to task-and-finish working groups or departments (where mobile has become embedded into departmental working practices), with remits which provide context for the strategic activity and dates for delivery. Recommendations for the membership of each task-and-finish group are suggested by the MTG in consultation with line managers and endorsed by the Assistant Director with responsibility for service development. More recently, membership was extended to the wider library community as a target under the communication strategic objective to widen library staff engagement with mobile initiatives.

The strategy in action

In the three phases of activity so far, progress has been made across the wide range of areas identified in the strategy. Services have been introduced or enhanced; the opportunities and challenges provided by technological advances have been explored; and future possibilities have been investigated. All of this activity has been guided by our strategic vision for mobile that has the user at its centre.

The following case studies describe a number of key initiatives that have been undertaken within the framework of the mobile strategy. These illustrate how the strategy has supported developments and how we have attempted to ensure that our mobile innovations are evidence based and focused on user needs.

Case study 1: getting the user perspective

Consideration of what users want should be at the centre of any strategy, but it is particularly important when trying to design new services in the ever-changing digital world. One of the core elements of the mobile strategy is the annual mobile survey, which is designed to gather user information on mobile device ownership, feedback on library mobile services and identification of barriers to access. The survey is devised and analysed by the Evidence Base for Mobile Group and is hosted on Survey Monkey, the online survey and questionnaire tool. It has ten questions and is designed to be completed quickly and easily by our users. It is primarily a quantitative survey, but there are a number of opportunities for respondents to give comments which provides rich qualitative data that enhances the analysis. The survey has run annually since 2011 and the evidence gathered has helped us to make key decisions and to evaluate our performance effectively.

Information on mobile device ownership

A key assumption of the library mobile strategy is that the resources and services we provide for mobile will be accessed by users on their own mobile devices. A strategy that is based on a 'bring your own device' (BYOD) policy can only succeed if we know more about our users and the devices they own. Collecting this information on a regular basis is particularly important in the mobile environment, where technological advances mean that new devices and updates to operating systems occur at an unprecedented rate. Linked to this are the timeframes that mobile internet service providers operate in, in terms of mobile device contracts, which means that many of our users change their devices every 18–24 months.

Responses from the three surveys undertaken so far reflect this ever-changing landscape. Smartphones are the most popular devices, with Apple and Android devices accounting for almost 60% of responses in the first two surveys, but closer to 80% in 2013. Other significant trends include the spectacular rise in the number of tablet owners, from 3% in 2010 to 33% in 2013, and the steady increase in the number of respondents who own more than one mobile device, from 11% in 2011 and 18% in 2012 to 33% in 2013. This data allows us to focus on delivering services to the most popular devices and operating systems.

Finding out what users want

The survey asks questions about the services we already have in place, but also seeks opinions on the types of services that our users would like in the future. In the first two surveys the top three services accessed by users on their mobile related to catalogue searching and accessing the most popular library account activities. When users were asked what services they would like to see in the future, in all three surveys the top three responses from a list of suggested additional library services were: read e-books, check out books and search for articles. These are services that we have been working towards since early 2011, but as yet have been unable to deliver as fully functional services because of technical and/or infrastructure barriers. Walsh argues that once you know what your users want and would find useful, you should go for the easiest options first. Tackling the easiest, but still desirable options first, can provide quick results and give the impression of being a mobile-friendly library (Walsh, 2012).

Challenges and barriers

As well as providing evidence of what our users want and expect, the surveys also provide feedback on services introduced and information on barriers to access and engagement. While services introduced so far have been well received, comments have also alerted us to problems that we were unaware of, but which clearly posed a barrier to access.

In both the first and second surveys, a significant number of users reported that they were experiencing problems accessing library information on their mobile devices. In the first survey, there was a specific problem for Android users gaining access to the library Wi-Fi infrastructure which we were able to resolve in consultation with colleagues from IT Services. In the second survey, problems accessing the Wi-Fi network in particular parts of the library building were reported by a number of respondents. In response to these comments, the MTG undertook a comprehensive survey of the library Wi-Fi network using devices running the operating systems most popular with our users. The results of the survey were passed to our senior management team and colleagues in IT Services and Estates and Buildings. After some detailed consultation, a plan for a major upgrade of library Wi-Fi system was integrated into a strategic bid being prepared for library refurbishment. That bid was successful and work completed in spring 2013.

Another challenge to the continuing success of the mobile strategy is communication. In all three surveys, a number of respondents have used the various 'other comments and suggestions' options to contribute their own ideas about library services for mobile. Somewhat disappointingly, these have provided evidence that information about the new services introduced by the library have not as yet been universally communicated to our users. As a result, the Mobile Marketing Sub-Group has been working on a number of imaginative initiatives in this area which are contributing towards our strategic aim of ensuring that mobile services are central to the user experience.

Conclusion

Results from the annual surveys add to our user-focused evidence base for mobile services and confirm that a significant and growing number of library users are mobile and have clear expectations about the availability of library services in this environment. While evidence shows that key targets identified in the strategy and services introduced so far are relevant, useful and appreciated by our users, it also provides us with information on the many challenges and barriers to mobile access that still exist.

The annual surveys have been an important aspect of determining our users' mobile expectations in respect of library services. Responding to them is equally important, even if this has to be done in an incremental way. The ongoing development of the library's mobile website provides an illustration of how a strategic approach to service delivery has allowed us to respond appropriately to user feedback in the constantly changing mobile environment. ■

Case study 2: delivery of a mobile website

The introduction of a mobile interface to the library catalogue had been one of the original drivers for the creation of the MTG. Preceding the development of the strategy, the introduction of such a service had been seen as an essential and achievable objective and was a key component in the original remit. Thomas (2012) argues that while a mobile strategy should encompass the broadest range of library services, it is important to identify the key priorities that can be met in the short term on a limited budget and set the foundation for future development.

Phase 1: introduction of a mobile catalogue

The MTG began by investigating a number of vendor-provided products. The AirPAC service,[3] which was developed by the providers of the library management system in use at Glasgow, was chosen largely because of the ease of integration with existing services. The product was installed during the first phase of the mobile strategy, providing a quick gain and thereby giving increased confidence to the group and the strategy. In addition to the catalogue search, the product provided access to library account functionality and allowed for the inclusion of limited information such as opening hours and contact details. As such, it was initially seen as a potential platform for the development of the mobile library website. However, evidence from the first annual mobile survey indicated that the limited functionality would not support our users' expectations for a mobile site. During the review and re-planning period at the end of the first phase of strategic activity, a decision was made to undertake a wider investigation of the options for creating a mobile website.

Phase 2: creation of mobile website

The content management system used to create the desktop version of the library website was not suitable for creating mobile content at that time. After investigation, it was decided to utilize the free open-source software iWebKit5 (http://snippetspace.com/portfolio/iwebkit). Testing indicated that this would be easy to implement and maintain. The content for the new mobile website was determined by evidence from the mobile surveys of library users. In response to questions about what services users would like to be able to access from a mobile device, 23% of respondents indicated they wanted to be able to search the catalogue and 29% wanted to be able to check their library account and renew books. The search and user account functionalities offered by the mobile catalogue product were separated out and offered as two direct links within the mobile website, thereby ensuring more direct access to the tasks that users want to undertake.

Another popular request was for journal article searching from a mobile device. At that time, the library's discovery service was not optimized for mobile; however, an interim response to this user demand was found by the investigations of the MTG E-resources Sub-group. Part of the remit of this group during the first two phases of strategic activity had been to identify mobile-friendly databases. The information was added to the library management system, from which listings of these databases could be dynamically generated within the library catalogue desktop site. With assistance from the vendors of the AirPAC product, the listings were optimized for small-screen display. The mobile-friendly URL for database listings was then added as a direct link within the mobile website.

Further services, such as real-time information on availability of PCs within the library building, a popular service available on desktops, were found to be compatible with small-screen devices and were also incorporated. The library mobile website, illustrated in Figure 7.1 on the following page, was launched on schedule at the end of Phase 2 with content that reflected some of our users' needs and expectations. Clearly there was still work to be done, not least in satisfying the 25% of survey respondents who want easy access to articles.

Phase 3: comprehensive mobile article search

Progress towards the successful delivery of this target has already been achieved as a result of the library's current review and trial of two discovery service products. Members of the MTG are involved in the discovery service review process and the importance of the mobile perspective ensures that this

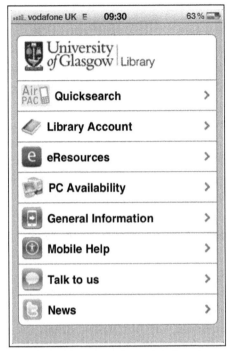

Figure 7.1 *Screenshot of University of Glasgow Library mobile website*
Source: University of Glasgow (reproduced with permission)

is a key factor in the choice of a library search and discovery system. A specific article search feature from one of these products has recently been incorporated within the mobile library website and is under review.

Conclusion

The successful and continuing, development of the mobile website is being achieved in an organized and incremental way in response to technological advances and user expectations. Current technological constraints are not seen as insurmountable barriers but as temporary obstacles which allow the opportunity to consider alternative, perhaps innovative, approaches. Features from different products have been combined to deliver the current mobile website and every element will be developed or replaced as user demand requires. ■

Supporting users

Providing services that our users want and expect is an important aspect of the mobile strategy, but supporting those users is equally important. Yee (2012, 13) notes that while most libraries are beginning to look at mobile services, they offer a 'casual approach' to staff up-skilling in this area. This was the approach assumed in the early stages of mobile developments at Glasgow. Initial engagement with library staff took the form of drop-in sessions to launch the strategy and the Live Lab concept. The Live Lab offers library staff hands-on opportunities to experience an extensive range of mobile devices across the most popular mobile operating platforms. Live Lab devices can be borrowed by library staff for use at their workspace, at home, at meetings or conferences. They can also be used within a dedicated physical space in the library. This facility has excellent Wi-Fi and 3G coverage and provides an environment in which mobile services can be explored, developed and tested collaboratively.

However, evidence from the Live Lab drop-in sessions indicated that, while there was enthusiasm among staff for mobile developments, familiarity with and knowledge of the technology was not widespread. One of the early priorities had been to develop a digital media skills plan for users which had been built on the assumption that library staff would be a key component in delivering this plan. In a change of focus, a new Digital Media Skills Sub-group was established with the specific remit of developing a programme to address this skills gap among library staff. The following case study illustrates how the strategic approach to service delivery allowed us to respond appropriately to new information.

Case study 3: library staff skills with '23 things mobile'

The Digital Media Skills Sub-group comprised six members from different areas of library service (subject liaison specialists, enquiry service and systems), each with differing levels of personal experience and knowledge in respect of mobile. The training model was considered and, while traditional approaches such as presentations and workshops were explored, it was felt that the success of any programme would be greater if the content were dynamic and designed to provide opportunities for participants to collaborate and participate actively. The '23 things' concept was identified from a programme that originated at the Public Library of Charlotte and Mecklenburg County in the USA (http://plcmcl2-things.blogspot.co.uk). This was a self-directed online learning programme, designed to allow staff to explore 23 different aspects of Web 2.0 technologies in a fun way and reward them for doing so. Participants were encouraged to work together and share experiences through their blogs. The Digital Media Skills Sub-group at Glasgow adopted this model, with some modifications, to create '23 things mobile'. The online content was created in the University VLE (virtual learning environment), illustrated in Figure 7.2 on the following page, and a separate blog was established. The course was scheduled to run over ten weeks and incorporated a 'Live Lab' event during week seven which was designed to give participants an opportunity for a collaborative and hands-on experience.

Identifying topics

A decision was taken at the outset that the programme would cover mobile

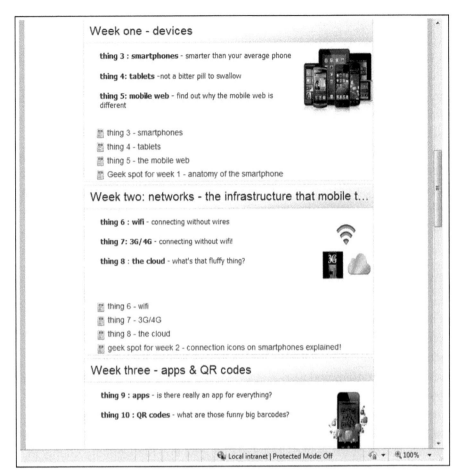

Figure 7.2   *Screenshot from '23 things mobile' course in the VLE*
Source: University of Glasgow (reproduced with permission)

technology in general, but library initiatives would be highlighted where relevant. The initial list of topics and the order in which they would be presented was revised a number of times. There were various reasons for this: some new 'things' were added as they were identified; it was necessary to ensure that participants could build on skills and information as they progressed through the course; and the basics needed to be covered before the Live Lab sessions, so that participants would get maximum benefit from the activities. The final list of 'things' was broadly grouped as:

- devices: smartphones, tablets, e-book readers
- networks: Wi-Fi, 3G, the Cloud
- applications: mobile web apps, QR codes, e-books

- communication: blogs, text/instant messaging, Twitter, e-mail
- sharing: Facebook, Google+, SharePoint
- fun stuff: Live Lab, music, photos, videos, gaming
- other: library mobile strategy, reflection on things learned.

Individual group members took responsibility for gathering information about specific topics and drafting content, which was then reviewed and revised collectively. The content was delivered within the VLE as a mixture of text, images and video. The varying levels of experience within the group probably reflected the range of experience within the library staff and ensured that the content was pitched at a suitable level, mostly introductory, but with opportunities for exploring more technical information. As a result of the course creation process, group members themselves came to understand better the range of technologies and the range of possibilities and so the production of the content was, in itself, the first instance of up-skilling library staff.

Pilot programme

Self-paced online learning was a new style of training programme within the library and it was decided to test the format with a pilot group of 25 participants. The course was introduced to the volunteer participants, who included members of the library senior management team, at a briefing session. Thereafter the content was made available online on a weekly basis. The participants' engagement with the programme was monitored both from usage statistics provided within the VLE and from interaction with the blog. The group had hoped for mutual support within the participating volunteers, with participants helping each other with questions and comments via the blog. Some participants were able to engage on this basis but some were more reluctant, with one commenting 'blogging still sends shivers down my spine!' However, the main difficulty experienced by some participants did not relate to the subject content but was more about allocating time, against competing work demands, to engage in a regular programme of online learning.

Participant feedback at the end of the course was gathered using a variety of mechanisms: via an online survey, a number of individual interviews and at a group prize-giving event. Apart from the issue of finding time, participants were very positive about the experience. The most popular aspect, which was enjoyed by 95% of respondents, was the Live Lab week, where small groups came together for a two-hour session to try out a range of practical activities. These included a QR code quiz, taking photos with either a smartphone or a tablet and uploading to the blog, comparing mobile and desktop sites and reading an interactive e-book. A typical comment from the survey was 'I like the idea of getting mixed groups of people together and letting them have the space to play around'. Course participants indicated that they had benefited and had 'a better understanding of how the library is using mobile technology and why it needs to'. When asked if they would recommend the course to a work colleague, 100% of respondents answered yes.

Programme roll-out

As a result of this success, the '23 things mobile' course has been approved by library senior management as a training requirement for all library staff during 2013. Where required, staff will be supported by line managers by having time (1 hour per week) specifically allocated to this training activity. The course has been shortened slightly and some course content has been updated (e.g., introduction of 4G). In addition and again as a result of feedback, the Live Lab event takes place earlier (week 5) in the programme. Interest in the course content has come from other departments within the University as well as libraries at other higher education institutions.

Since participating in the '23 things mobile' pilot, a number of staff have been inspired to become more engaged with the library's mobile initiatives. Some answered the call to volunteer to join MTG activities during Phase 3 and all of the current MTG sub-groups now include members of library staff who had not previously been involved with the library's mobile initiatives. Others have offered to act as 'buddies' or mentors to the next group of participants taking part in the '23 things mobile' training programme. Hopefully, this will offer encouragement to the new participants but also provide an opportunity for the original participants to keep their skills and knowledge updated as the course content is revised to reflect new mobile developments. Chatterton (2010) suggests that encouraging early adopters of innovation to become buddies or mentors to pass on knowledge to other staff is a simple but effective approach to transferring expertise, knowledge and know-how.

Conclusion

In a period where mobile devices are beginning to define the everyday experiences of our users, a skilled workforce who are confident and engaged with mobile technologies will be vital to the future success of not only the library mobile strategy but of the service generally. Yee (2012) concludes that the challenge for libraries is to have a pool of skilled staff ready to take on emerging new roles and to have strategic plans prioritized, as technology timeframes are very short. ▩

Conclusion

This chapter describes the University of Glasgow Library's strategic approach to service development in the ever-changing digital environment. There are a number of key elements that have contributed to the ongoing success of our mobile strategy, but these would be applicable to any large project. It is essential to have an overall vision for the project with high-level aims that are aligned to organizational strategic priorities. This will help to gain senior management buy-in, which is essential as they have the ability to command the budgets and resources necessary to make strategic goals a reality. The strategic framework must be flexible and adaptable to allow a response to new information, changing circumstances and technological advances. Acknowledge that there is a fear of change and understand that not every initiative will be deliverable. Understand your users and find out what services they want and expect. Establish open and ongoing dialogue with both library staff and users of the service about strategic objectives and priorities and encourage active participation in the process.

In our experience of developing services for mobile, we have found that taking the strategic approach has kept us focused, motivated and able to continually develop our services and respond to the challenges of working in this rapidly changing digital environment.

Notes

1   www.ericsson.com/mobility-report.
2   www.jiscinfonet.ac.uk/Infokits/strategy.
3   www.iii.com/products/airpac.shtml.

References

Belshaw, D. (2010) *Mobile and Wireless Technologies Review*,
    http://mobilereview.jiscpress.org.
Chatterton, P. (2010) *Sustaining and Embedding Innovations: a good practice guide*,
    https://sustainembed.pbworks.com/w/page/31632855/Welcome.
Coalition for Networked Information (2012) *Multiple Devices and Platforms:*

institutional strategies, CNI's Executive Roundtable, 2 April, 2012, www.cni.org/executive-roundtable-reports/multiple-devices-and-platforms-institutional-strategies.

comScore (2013) *UK Digital Future in Focus 2013: key insights from 2012 and what they mean for the coming year*, www.comscore.com/Insights.

Jisc (2009, updated 2012) *Managing Strategic Activity InfoKit*, www.jiscinfonet.ac.uk/infokits/managing-strategic-activity.

Jisc (2010) *JISC Strategy infoKit*, www.jiscinfonet.ac.uk/Infokits/strategy.

Jisc (2012) *Defining and Articulating Your Vision, Mission and Values*, www.jiscinfonet.ac.uk/infokits/mission-vision-values.

Johnson, L. and Adams, S. (2011) *Technology Outlook for UK Tertiary Education 2011–2016: an NMC Horizon Report regional analysis*, The New Media Consortium, Austin, TX, www.nmc.org/pdf/2011-Technology-Outlook-UK.pdf.

Power, M. (2012) *Delivering Web to Mobile*, Jisc Observatory Techwatch Report, http://observatory.jisc.ac.uk/docs/delivering-web-to-mobile.pdf.

Showers, B. (2012) Transforming Library Services with Mobile Technology, *Research Information*, 4 December, www.researchinformation.info/news/news_story.php?news_id=1056.

Thomas, L. C. (2012) Next Step Mobile: strategy, services, & PRM, *Journal of Web Librarianship*, **6** (2), 133–5.

Walsh, A. (2012) *Using Mobile Technology to Deliver Library Services: a handbook*, Facet Publishing, London.

Yee, A. (2012) Mobile Technology: academic libraries in Australia and beyond. In Rutherford, B. (ed.), *VALA 2012 Proceedings, Melbourne, Australia, 6–9 February 2012*, 1–18, http://researchbank.rmit.edu.au/eserv/rmit:15297/n2006032152.pdf.

CHAPTER 8

'You might also be interested in . . .': improving discovery through recommendations

Lisa Charnock and Joy Palmer

Introduction

'There aren't enough books in the library' is a common student complaint. With undergraduate library research largely driven by reading lists, the frustrations of unavailable titles and long reservation lists are a big source of student dissatisfaction and this is often reflected in their responses to the UK annual National Student Survey. As some UK students pay more for their university education, their expectations rise accordingly and this means that libraries are constantly being challenged to meet the ever-shifting demands of their users. As Bevan points out, 'students will begin to wonder why, when they pay up to £9000 in tuition fees a year, they cannot access the books they have been told are essential' (Bevan, 2012).

In their White Paper, Capita stress that 'innovation is the key to meeting and exceeding student expectations' (Capita, 2013) and one of the ways that libraries can innovate is by offering recommendations. By making the most of technology and using the data at their fingertips, libraries can offer new routes to resource discovery and reveal underused or hidden library materials through book recommendations. These kinds of recommendations, generated by the tracking of reading habits and purchases, are now a common feature on commercial and social websites such as Amazon, LibraryThing and Goodreads, but this is a trend which is still relatively rare in UK academic library catalogues. However, universities and colleges have access to a wealth of activity data that can give insights into user behaviour and help to develop these kinds of services.

With a primary focus on continuing work at Mimas, The University of Manchester, to explore how library circulation data can be aggregated and used to support research, this chapter examines how institutions in the UK are now exploiting their activity data to enhance discoverability and enable wider use of resources by surfacing and recommending library resources that users might not have ordinarily found. It will also attempt to answer whether book recommendations in library catalogues can help to alleviate student frustrations around finding resources in the library.

Recommendations and activity data

Activity data is the record of any user action (Jisc, 2011) and the powerful potential of this data to support personalized search is well established in the commercial sector. This use of activity data is commonly known as adaptive personalization, defined as 'where the availability of options, interface, access or functionality [and provision of other personalized results] is based upon knowledge about users gained from tracking user activity and/or other sources of user information' (van Harmelen, 2008).

Customers of sites such as Amazon expect to see personalized suggestions for products they may wish to purchase, but higher education institutions could be said to have fallen behind the trend in this area. In library terms, activity data such as book loans have been used to provide Amazon-style recommendations to users, but in an analysis of library catalogues, Wakeling et al. (2012, 142) found that 'the number of OPACs offering recommendations to library users is extremely low'. A number of libraries have made developments in this area, for example through the implementation of LibraryThing for Libraries, but few are offering recommendations through their catalogues at the item level.

However, recent years have seen academic libraries begin to recognize the possibilities. Through grassroots projects, commercial partnerships and research and development, libraries are now producing evidence to suggest that, by using the data at their disposal, they can develop popular services for students and increase usage of their valuable collections. As Kay and van Harmelen point out in their report on the potential benefits of activity data, through their access to data and intelligence from a variety of sources such as library management systems (LMS), higher education institutions are in an advantageous position to 'understand and support users more effectively and to manage resources more efficiently' (Kay and van Harmelen, 2013). One of the ways that libraries can do this is to personalize the information search experience and by 'providing recommendations for resources that support learning and research by using the results of other people's searches that relate to the users' current search' (Jisc, 2011).

In the UK, Huddersfield University Library has been a pioneer in this area and has been exploiting the potential of its activity data through its library catalogue since 2006. By using its circulation data to develop and implement an in-house recommender, it found that new borrowing patterns were beginning to emerge. It found evidence to suggest that recommendations could result in increased borrowing and, more significantly, more borrowing of related materials. As Library Systems Manager Dave Pattern explains:

> Since adding the features in early 2006, we've seen a year-on-year increase in the range of titles being borrowed . . . Not only are students borrowing more widely than before, they're also borrowing more books than before.
>
> Pattern, 2009.

Pattern clarifies that the range of unique titles borrowed increased from 65,000 to 80,000 per year and the average number of books borrowed had increased from 14 to around 16 books per student per year (Harrop et al., 2010a, 30).

Following on from this, the 2009 Jisc-funded MOSAIC (Making Our Scholarly Activity Information Count) programme was commissioned to 'investigate the possibilities for exploiting the user activity and resource use data that might currently or potentially be made available through Higher Education systems to benefit libraries, national services and their users' (Harrop et al., 2010a, 93). Working with Mimas and academic library and learning services across the UK to aggregate data and make it available for reuse and experimentation, the project found strong interest and enthusiasm from institutions which saw potential for supporting discovery and personalization. Although this project also identified clear issues, from data privacy to technical difficulties in extracting the data, perhaps most compelling is the evidence from library users themselves. In the MOSAIC evaluation, 90% of participants said that they would be interested in seeing what resources other students, lecturers or researchers were using to help them to get a better picture of what is available in the library, to aid the retrieval of relevant resources and to help them find resources for their coursework (Harrop et al., 2010b, 37).

This enthusiasm was echoed more recently in the Open University Recommendations Improve the Search Experience (OURISE) project, which used attention data to provide recommendations through their EBSCO Discovery Solution. Although the project team was unable to prove whether the new functionality had increased usage of resources, they did find that their users were positive about the concept of recommendations and, more importantly, they state that 'comments in the evaluations would seem to indicate that users are getting some resources they would not otherwise have found' (Open University, 2011).

If students are often unhappy that the books they want to access are out on loan, then could a recommender built upon circulation data from the usage of academic library users themselves lead students towards alternative titles and give them a bigger picture of what is available? And could this simple addition to catalogues and search tools offer students and researchers a route to information that would be otherwise hidden to them? The experience of Huddersfield and the Open University suggests that this could be the case and this gives us a clear message that this is something library users are interested in and would use.

Aggregating library circulation data

In 2011 the UK National Data Centre, Mimas, began exploring recommendations and circulation data through Copac, a UK national, academic and specialist union catalogue service. They were keen to explore whether library circulation data could be used to support library users by surfacing underused 'long-tail' library materials. The Copac Activity Data project aggregated the data of five academic libraries (the Universities of Manchester, Huddersfield, Lincoln, Sussex and Cambridge) to explore the potential to develop an application programming interface (API) based on shared circulation data. An API (a machine-to-machine interface that makes it possible to share data and functionality between different pieces of software) was an obvious choice for this project, as they wanted to develop something that could be plugged into any library catalogue, yet would generate recommendations using data held on the servers at Mimas in Manchester.

Figures 8.1 and 8.2 on the following pages illustrate the API working in the test websites of The University of Manchester Library and Copac.

Surfacing the academic long tail

As mentioned above, the initial aim of the Copac Activity Data work was to surface underused 'long-tail' library materials, but what is meant by 'long-tail' in this context? In short, many library texts are not being borrowed.

Figure 8.1 *Recommendations in The University of Manchester Library Catalogue*
Source: The University of Manchester Library (reproduced with permission)

Dempsey (2006) points out that libraries contain deep collections of materials, yet cites a study that found that 10% of books accounted for about 90% of circulations in two research libraries. This is, perhaps, unsurprising in an environment where student demand is driven by the academic reading list – a situation which is itself problematic. Academic teaching staff and librarians repeatedly advocate the importance of wider reading but is this a message fully endorsed by all library users? Research by Stokes and Martin suggests not. They found that, although tutors viewed the reading list as a springboard and a tool for providing guidance, students were unlikely to look beyond the list and instead exhibited a means–end approach to research. Indeed, within their sample, '67% at level one said they consulted no more than four items and 47% claimed to consult no more than two or three items' (Stokes and Martin, 2008, 119).

This is clearly a problem that cannot be solved solely through the introduction of recommendations but recommendations can offer a simple way, as Dempsey suggests, to ensure that the full breadth of materials are

Figure 8.2   *Recommendations in Copac*
Source: Copac (reproduced with permission)

readily and easily visible to users. The assumption was that if libraries were willing to share their circulation data, we could build a rich picture of borrowing patterns from a range of institutions, one that would not be skewed to reflect one institution's reading lists or research specialism. By doing this, the data could be used to lead students and researchers towards those wider reading materials and beyond the head of the tail.

What are the benefits of activity data and recommendations?

So why might this approach be beneficial for library users? For researchers and in particular humanities researchers, serendipity and browsing are a key part of their research strategy. Palmer describes this as centrifugal searching, describing an information-gathering process that is 'relatively open-ended, moving outward from lead to lead' (Palmer, 2005, 1146).

At Mimas, ongoing in-house user research is conducted with students and researchers and the findings substantiate this. The students and researchers in the focus groups share many patterns of behaviour. They are inclined to cherry-pick and follow somewhat erratic trails and paths to find the information they need. They repeatedly emphasize the importance of serendipity in their information searching and they also speak of their anxiety that they might miss important resources that would help them in their work.

For these users, a simple recommender function can offer new possibilities. This kind of adaptive personalization can support humanities users in their preferred mode of discovery, powering centrifugal searching and discovery through serendipity. By using activity data as the backbone of the tool, this functionality could provide trails and new routes to discovery based on actual use and disciplinary contexts. In other words, the recommendations would reflect patterns of real usage, and how other users with similar academic interests are aggregating texts. This is particularly useful for finding conceptually related groupings of texts that cut across different disciplines and which will not ordinarily sit together in a standard results set.

Benefits to library users: the Copac Activity Data evaluations

There is some evidence to suggest that recommendations can help to alleviate some of the frustrations around the perceived lack of texts in the library. As mentioned above, the introduction of recommendations to the University of Huddersfield library catalogue resulted in increased borrowing from a broader range of relevant materials, and the evaluations for the Copac Activity Data project also revealed some interesting insights. Five focus groups were held with a random selection of humanities postgraduate researchers and undergraduate students from The University of Manchester and Manchester Metropolitan University. Three main questions were considered:

1 Does the recommender suggest books that are logical and useful?
2 Does it suggest items that you were previously unaware of?
3 Would you be likely to borrow the suggested books?

As we were interested in whether the recommender would increase the visibility of hidden items, library users were asked to conduct searches in their area of expertise and rate the recommendations returned by the API working in Copac and The University of Manchester library catalogue. The first postgraduate focus group participants completed 42 searches. Encouragingly, 78% of these searches returned at least one recommendation (and usually many more) that was considered to be useful and they indicated that they would consider borrowing over 50% of the items. However, it was clear that in some cases the recommendations were of little relevance. In the second postgraduate group, following a little tweaking of the API, 25 searches were conducted. This time, 92% of the searches from Manchester's library catalogue and 100% of searches from Copac returned at least one item the user thought would be useful and, overall, 56% of the recommendations would be likely to be borrowed.

In terms of whether the recommendations were surfacing hidden items, the results were mixed. In some cases the recommender returned items that were not familiar to the users, but the perceived relevance of the recommendations suffered as a result of their obscurity. In other cases, participants indicated that recommendations were relevant but would not necessarily be borrowed. Reasons for this varied. In some cases it was simply that they had borrowed the book before, in some cases the year of publication indicated that the book could be out of date and in some cases their area of research was so niche it wasn't specifically useful to them but they would deem it 'useful to others in their field'. So what does this mean for recommendations? It could be argued that there is a place for both known and unknown texts to be surfaced by a recommender. On the one hand, familiarity with the recommended texts inspires confidence in the results while new and unfamiliar suggestions offer the possibilities of new material.

For the undergraduates, it was clear that the recommendations offered them an alternative to their reading lists. As expected, frustration about the lack of available resources was high on their list of complaints and their reading lists were seen as a vital route to the resources they should be accessing. However, they saw the recommender as having the potential to give them another way of finding out about connected useful resources if there were limited copies of their chosen books available to them. Here are just some of the comments from undergraduate students at Manchester Metropolitan University who tested the recommender in Copac:

> It would be useful as I had to read a book for a topic area and when we got the topic area there were already 25 reservations on the book, so if I could click on

something and see what the person who did this last year read, that would be very useful.

As undergraduates it is useful to us, because there are only so many books in the library from the reading list and if they are out then you get stuck, so you need recommendations.

If you search for a keyword in a library catalogue sometimes you only get one book, but with the recommender you get loads, which is really good, that I thought was useful. It gives you recommendations in the topic area, not just in the title.

Perhaps most importantly, in all of the Copac Activity Data user testing groups and interviews, the participants found at least one recommendation that they would consider borrowing. All of the participants reported that the recommender would be a welcome addition to library catalogues and they gave their resolute approval for their data to be collected and used for this purpose.

A number of academic staff were also interviewed and for this audience the recommender returned legitimate and useful suggestions, which they indicated could be used to develop reading lists. Indeed, one academic commented that 'this is a seriously useful addition to Copac . . . it's great for a reading list developer but this is a major advantage for students'.

The Copac Activity Data team also spoke to nine academic liaison librarians from across the UK to elicit their views and to ask for their evaluation of the recommender working in the Copac search interface. Encouragingly, there was a lot of support for the development of recommendations. With budgets and spending increasingly under scrutiny, it is important to demonstrate the value of library collections and increasing usage of collections is key. By surfacing stock not included on reading lists, recommendations could help front-line staff to point their users towards worthwhile items and encourage the borrowing of items they might not have considered. As one interviewee stated, 'anything that encourages students to look more widely is a good thing'.

In addition, some new ideas emerged from the discussions related to the introduction of recommendations based on aggregated circulation data from other libraries. There was interest in the benefits of sharing information between libraries and suggestions that this could help with collection development itself. For example, using this data could inform alternative purchases for out-of-date or out-of-print texts and could also be a quick and easy way to find relevant items for purchase based on use at other institutions.

What are the issues?

Although recommendations do seem to improve student perceptions of library resources, using activity data to generate these recommendations does raise some issues and questions.

Data privacy

In order to develop recommenders, vast amounts of user data are accessed and processed and user anonymity must be protected at all stages. The Jisc Activity Data project discusses this in detail (Jisc, 2011) and proposes a number of solutions to ensure that data use does not disrespect the users' right to privacy.

Throughout the Copac Activity Data project, students and researchers were interviewed to elicit their views on this issue. Although it is possible to process and anonymize data to ensure privacy, there is a small possibility that a postgraduate student studying a niche topic area could, potentially, be identified by their patterns of borrowing. Moreover, users could have concerns about their data being collected this way. We were therefore surprised by the responses. No one expressed any concern about the collection of activity data and its use in the recommender. In fact, most participants assumed this data was collected anyway and encouraged its use if it was for the development of a tool that would help them to research more effectively and efficiently. Although they initially had slight concerns about their reading habits being tracked, these were outweighed by the perceived benefits of the tool. Many, however, were clear that their trust was linked to the fact that this was a non-commercial, publicly funded project working within universities and they were less comfortable with commercial companies tracking and using their data. While potential privacy issues cannot be ignored, the initial conversations indicate that users trust libraries to respect their privacy and to only use their data in an ethical and constructive way, as these quotes from the focus group attendees illustrate:

> It's not as if it is being used for commercial gain, then what is the issue?
> Postgraduate researcher at The University of Manchester

> I would benefit from everyone else's borrowing as they are benefiting from mine, so I haven't got a problem.
> Undergraduate at Manchester Metropolitan University

Quality and relevance

Another potential issue arises from the quality of the recommendations themselves, as a recommendation engine is only as good as the recommendations it proposes. As Kop asks, 'could we ever trust a machine, even though it is tweaked by humans, to find really useful information for us?' (Kop, 2012, 5).

In the Copac Activity Data projects, it became clear that, although many of the suggestions generated were useful and relevant, some were seen to be tangential or too generic by many of the research participants. Through all of the interviews and focus groups with students, librarians and academics, users found results that were unexpected and, for some postgraduate researchers their areas of interest were so niche that there was not enough circulation data to return appropriate results.

However, this unpredictability was not an issue for many users and was accepted as a characteristic of recommenders in general. Although some of the results were mixed, participants did not see this as an issue as long as the recommender returned at least one item that was relevant.

The non-linear approach to research favoured by many scholars in the humanities and the circuitous cherry-picking approach were both employed in their responses to the recommendations. An academic lecturer interviewed during the project stated that 'the editions and recommendations offered some interesting trails', emphasizing the continued importance of serendipity in the world of research. André et al. suggest that the 'success of serendipitous discovery is not just the find itself, but being able or willing to do something with it' (André et al., 2009). The interviews with librarians seem to support this view. There was a consensus that no recommender would produce 100% perfect results for every search and it was suggested that users would use their discretion to evaluate the results; indeed, one commented that 'Amazon does this too . . . You take what you want from it'. In other words, a recommender can make suggestions, but what one researcher considers a hidden gem, another will consider an irrelevance. The overall agreement was that the appearance of the occasional irrelevant suggestion should not impede the development or implementation of these tools.

Provenance and trust

The majority of the research participants had used Amazon's recommender function and all would welcome a similar function in the library, but it is important here to make a distinction between commercial products and recommendations built on circulation data. The lack of commercial interest did add a level of trust and the academic interviewees saw a recommender based on activity data as more refined and suited to their work than other products. Moreover, the findings of the OURISE project evaluation suggest that trust and quality are key concerns for library users, particularly postgraduate researchers. Their evaluations concluded that students were interested in the provenance of the recommendations and were unsure whether to trust the suggestions if they did not understand why the items had been recommended. As the project team explain: 'There is a critical element of trust that is needed. You could characterize it as "I don't know whether to trust this information until I know more about who or where it comes from".'

So is it the case that recommendations can improve the search experience only if users have awareness of the origins of those suggestions? Wakeling et al. (2012, 2) suggest that 'in order for recommendations to properly aid information discovery, users need to be convinced of both the efficacy of the system and the credibility of those other users indirectly responsible for the recommendations'. This is where activity data can play a key role.

MOSAIC rejected the argument that recommendation functionality should be entrusted to 'web scale' operations such as Google and Amazon because 'the UK HE sector has the ability to gather and use "context" data . . . which would uniquely add value for students, the course designer and the library manager'. User research on the OURISE and MOSAIC projects suggests that library users would be interested in seeing recommendations generated from the borrowing patterns of other people on their course, people who have studied similar areas in previous years and people on similar courses at another university. By combining data from LMS, virtual learning environments and other institutional systems, this kind of recommendation is possible and other projects have investigated the possibilities of merging this data. By merging different datasets, users have a trusted route to resources they may not otherwise have found.

Introducing recommendations

Introducing recommendations can bring benefits for libraries and their users, but, as discussed, this functionality is not yet common in library catalogues. Is this something that can be implemented easily by libraries?

As with the example of the University of Huddersfield, by collecting and interrogating activity data in-house this kind of functionality can be implemented by individual institutions. However, it is fair to argue that conflicting priorities in libraries can mean that this kind of work may not be given precedence. Throughout the Copac project, we spoke to library managers and it was clear that without clear articulation of the benefits, leveraging activity data is unlikely to be high on the priority list. As Palmer points out, 'While within our community a significant amount of momentum is building in this area, our meetings with librarians indicate that the "why should I care?" and more to the point "why should I make this a priority?" questions are not adequately answered' (Palmer, 2011). The Jisc Activity Data Programme has made progress in this area and has attempted to promote the advantages through the resulting 'Exploiting activity data in the academic environment' website (www.activitydata.org), but more work is needed to communicate these benefits more widely.

One of the main issues is appropriate technical support, which is not uniformly available or easily accessible by all libraries. Clearly, introducing a recommender to an LMS will require sustained technical resource and skills, particularly in the initial set-up period. Recent work has also sought to alleviate the issues around the technical processes needed to use activity data. The collation of 'recipes' for extracting, processing and presenting data for a range of LMS means that new adopters can benefit from the experience of the early adopters.

Returning to activity data, the momentum shows no sign of waning. For recommender functionality, the Copac Activity Data project delivered a working prototype that was tested successfully in two library catalogue systems. At time of writing, the API is still under development, but it will eventually allow developers within academic institutions to draw from it to provide recommendations within their catalogues. While this project was experimental, aiming to understand the issues and perceived value of this approach, it is anticipated that the work will be taken further to develop a shared community service for the UK via the Jisc Library Analytics and Metrics (JiscLAMP) project (Jisc, Mimas and the University of Huddersfield, 2013). JiscLAMP looks to the bigger picture, taking the view that, if libraries think strategically and capture a range of data, these can be harnessed to improve and develop personalized services and tailored student support. Moreover, it can also help to demonstrate impact, as evidenced by the University of Huddersfield which, in its Library Impact Data project, combined library data with information on retention data and UCAS points and found a statistically significant relationship between library resource use and level of degree result (Stone, Pattern and Ramsden, 2012).

Beyond recommendations – the bigger picture

JiscLAMP is looking at the broader landscape to explore the possibilities for capturing and visualizing not just circulation and issue statistics, but also e-resource usage data, PC log-ins within the library, library gate entry, student records and UCAS points. Beyond recommender functionality, activity data is proving to be a valuable asset for libraries. From early experiments, the potential of activity data is now being fully realized and institutions are recognizing the importance of capitalizing on the data they collect every day.

In November 2012 Jisc worked with Research Libraries UK (RLUK), SCONUL and Mimas to run a community-wide survey within the UK academic library sector. The aim was to gauge the potential demand for data analytics services that could enhance business intelligence at the institutional level and so support strategic decision-making within libraries. There is an ongoing debate on the importance of analytics to academic libraries now and in the future and the potential demand for a shared service in this area. One option which is currently under development, with a prototype being explored as part of the JiscLAMP project, is a shared service that centrally ingests and processes raw usage data and data visualizations back to local institutions.

The survey elicited response from 66 UK HE institutions and asked a wide range of questions to gauge demand and also the strategic drivers within institutions, including whether the following functions might be useful: automated provision of analytics demonstrating the relationship between student attainment and resource/library usage within institutions; automated provision of analytics demonstrating e-resource and collections (e.g. monographs) usage according to demographics (e.g. discipline, year, age, nationality, grade); and resource recommendation functions for discovery services. Perhaps not surprisingly, the overwhelming response was positive – these tools would be valuable, yes (over 90% 'yes' rate each time). Respondents indicated which strategic drivers were behind their responses, e.g. supporting research excellence, enhancing the student experience, collection management, creating business efficiencies and demonstrating value for money. What was found (based on the sample) was that the dominant driver was 'enhancing the student experience', closely followed by the ability to demonstrate value for money and then the ability to support research excellence.

There also appeared to be a strong willingness to share business intelligence data with the wider community, so long as this is done in a carefully managed way that does not potentially expose too much about individual institutions. Understandably there was far more hesitation over sharing UCAS and student data than other forms of transactional data.

Are analytics a *current* strategic priority for institutions? Only nine respondents said 'yes, it is a top priority at the present moment', with 39 stating that it was important but not essential. But this changed significantly when respondents were asked to forecast five years ahead. The majority indicated that this would be a top priority for their library and institution within that timeframe. Nonetheless, undertaking this kind of work at the institutional and national level will be highly challenging. Perhaps most challenging is the complex variation in institutional structures and processes for decision-making. When respondents were asked which individuals at their institution would be the senior decision makers in making activity data available for reuse, while many indicated that this would be the purview of Library Directors and IT Directors, there were just as many different responses citing Vice-Chancellors, Registrars, Deputy Vice-Chancellors, the University Planning Office or the Director of Finance. Other potential barriers to sharing include concerns over data privacy and sharing business intelligence and the survey results revealed a mixed picture in terms of concerns over data quality, lack of technical expertise and the fact that there are strong competing demands at the institutional level. Clearly the community remains in the relatively early and experimental stages of this work, but the strategic drivers are extremely strong and the JiscLAMP project will help identify on a practical level what is feasible.

Conclusions

So, can recommendations built on circulation data reduce student frustrations and support research by surfacing underused library materials through search? It is, perhaps, too early to say with any confidence but encouraging results from institutions such as the University of Huddersfield, the Open University and Mimas suggest that it could become a tool that would help library users to follow alternative paths and borrow more widely. Support for recommender functionality among the users we spoke to was unanimous and early indications show that a recommender based on circulation data does return suggestions that are interesting, relevant and in some cases, not previously known to the users. The Copac

Activity Data project recognizes that library circulation data alone will only offer a partial solution to discoverability. For example, reference texts and e-books are non-circulating, and with e-books becoming more prevalent, this data will be needed in the future. However, evaluations suggest that a tool based on the owned data is something that researchers will welcome, and perhaps trust more than a commercial alternative.

These experiments have also opened new discussions about how activity data can improve the student experience and support decision-making in the library. As these questions are explored, and as more libraries and institutions open and collect data of all kinds, this opens up exciting new opportunities to develop library services and understand the users better.

References and further reading

André, P., Schraefel, M. C., Tevan, J. and Dumais, S. T. (2009) Discovery Is Never By Chance: designing for (un)serendipity. In *Proceedings of ACM Creativity & Cognition, 26–30 October 2009*, Berkeley, CA.

Bevan, N. (2012) Preliminary to Reading, *Times Higher Education*, 23 February, www.timeshighereducation.co.uk/419086.article.

Capita (2013) *Protecting Library Services* www.capita-softwareandmanagedservices. co.uk/news/Pages/protecting_library_services_white_paper.aspx

Copac (2011) *Copac Innovations: activity data*, http://copac.ac.uk/innovations/activity-data/?page_id=227.

Dempsey, L. (2006) Libraries and the Long Tail: some thoughts about libraries in a network age, *D-Lib Magazine*, **12** (4), www.dlib.org/dlib/april06/dempsey/04dempsey.html.

Flanders, D. and Ramsay, M. (2012) *The Advantages of APIs: how to jump the information gap*, www.jisc.ac.uk/publications/reports/2012/advantages-of-api.aspx#2.

Harrop, H., Kay, D., Chad, K., van Harmelen, M., Miller, P. and Pattern, D. (2010a) *The JISC MOSAIC Project (Making Our Scholarly Activity Information Count): final report*, www.sero.co.uk/mosaic/100322_MOSAIC_Final_Report_v7_FINAL.pdf.

Harrop, H., Kay, D., Chad, K., van Harmelen, M., Miller, P. and Pattern, D. (2010b) *The JISC MOSAIC Project (Making Our Scholarly Activity Information Count): final report appendices*, www.jisc.ac.uk/media/documents/progreammes/e-learningcapital/mosaicfinalreport.doc.

Jisc (2011) *Exploiting Activity Data in the Academic Environment*, www.activitydata.org.

Jisc, Mimas and the University of Huddersfield (2013) *JiscLAMP – Shedding Light on Library Data and Metrics*, http://jisclamp.mimas.ac.uk.

Kay, D. and van Harmelen, M. (2013) *Activity Data: delivering benefits from the data deluge*, www.jisc.ac.uk/publications/reports/2012/activity-data-delivering-benefits.aspx.

Kop, R. (2012) The Unexpected Connection: serendipity and human mediation in networked learning, *Educational Technology & Society*, **15** (2), 2–11, www.ifets.info/journals/15_2/2.pdf.

Open University (2011) *RISE (Recommendations Improve the Search Experience) Blog*, www.open.ac.uk/blogs/RISE/2011/05/19/search-focus-groups.

Palmer, C. L. (2005) Scholarly Work and the Shaping of Digital Access, *Journal of the American Society for Information Science and Technology*, **56** (11), 1140–53, http://onlinelibrary.wiley.com/doi/10.1002/asi.20204/pdf.

Palmer, J. (2011) Final blog post, *Copac Activity Data Blog*, 1 August, http://copac.ac.uk/innovations/activity-data/?p=187.

Pattern, D. (2009) Self-plagiarism is Style, *Dave Pattern's Blog*, ILI 2009 presentation, http://daveyp.wordpress.com/2009/10/15/ili-2009-presentation.

Stokes, P. and Martin, L. (2008) Reading Lists: a study of tutor and student perceptions, expectations and realities, *Studies in Higher Education*, **33** (2), 113–25, http://dx.doi.org/10.1080/03075070801915874.

Stone, G., Pattern, D. and Ramsden, B. (2012) Library Impact Data Project, *SCONUL Focus*, **54**, 25–8, www.sconul.ac.uk/sites/default/files/documents/8_0.pdf.

van Harmelen, M. (2008) *Developing Personalisation for the Information Environment Project 1: personalisation and Web 2.0 – final report*, http://repository.jisc.ac.uk/id/eprint/437.

Wakeling, S. (2012) The User-centered Design of a Recommender System for a Universal Library Catalogue. In *Proceedings of RecSys 2012, 9–13 September, Dublin, Ireland*, http://wanlab.poly.edu/recsys12/recsys/p337.pdf.

Wakeling, S., Clough, P., Sen, B. and Connaway, L. (2011) If We Build It, Will They Come? Recommendations and WorldCat, *Proceedings of the American Society for Information Science & Technology*, **48** (1), 1–3, http://onlinelibrary.wiley.com/doi/10.1002/meet.145.v48:1/issuetoc.

Wakeling, S. Clough, P., Sen, B. and Connaway, L. (2012) 'Readers Who Borrowed This Also Borrowed? . . . ?': recommender systems in UK libraries, *Library Hi Tech*, **30** (1), 134–50, www.emeraldinsight.com/journals.htm?articleid=17020849.

CHAPTER 9

Libraries and international branch campuses in the digital environment

Moira Bent

The author wishes to acknowledge the contribution made to this chapter by Karen Senior (formerly Head of Library, University of Bolton).

Introduction

In a globalized economy, as institutions driven by the need to maximize their income extend their reach outside their country's borders to establish outposts around the world, what are the challenges faced by academic libraries? Does our digitally rich learning environment lead to unrealistic expectations of library support or is it an enabler to a more consistent level of access? Although much has been written about transnational education (TNE) in general, as Wang and Tremblay (2009) have recognized, there is a lack of information in the current literature about how academic libraries support their domestic students studying abroad. A review of the literature also reveals a lack of research on the ways in which the growth of overseas campuses impacts upon academic libraries on the home campus. This chapter will try to answer some of the fundamental questions posed on this topic through evidence gained from working with a university's international branch campuses (IBCs). It will illustrate some of the benefits and challenges of engaging in international activities, particularly in a digital environment. It is essential that digital capabilities are used to their greatest effect in order to fully realize the ambitions and plans of countries such as Australia, where it is government policy to grow the international student population through overseas enterprises.

Alongside examples from around the world, a case study based on the experience of a UK institution, Newcastle University, will be used throughout the chapter to illustrate specific points. Newcastle University in Singapore is an academic alliance with Singapore Institute of Technology, offering academic programmes, hosted in two local polytechnics, with staff and students based on either one of the sites. In total 23 Newcastle University academic staff, 38 adjunct staff (local Singaporean guest lecturers) and over 500 students are based in Singapore, supported by 10 administrative staff. Students have physical access to the two local polytechnic libraries and digital access to Newcastle resources, supported at a distance by Newcastle-based library staff.

Transnational education and the international branch campus

There are many different ways in which students can be viewed as 'international'; they may have travelled from their home country to take a degree at a university in a different country, or they may take time away from the home university to study in a different country for a defined period. Students may undertake project or dissertation research in other countries or participate in field trips. In all these cases, students will have a primary tie to the original institution and may be expected to have some experience and expectation of the home library service, both physical and digital. These instances are features of transnational education, which has been defined by the Organisation of Economic Co-operation and Development (OECD) as 'All types of higher education study programmes, or sets of courses of study, or educational services (including those of distance education) in which the learners are located in a country different from the one where the awarding institution is based' (Council of Europe, 2002). A simpler definition might be 'education provision from one country offered in another' (British Council, 2008).

A branch campus in another country, however, implies a more specific definition. The Office for Borderless Higher Education (OBHE) describes an international branch campus (IBC) as

> a higher education institution that is located in another country from the institution which either originated it or operates it, with some physical presence in the host country and which awards at least one degree in the host country that is accredited in the country of the originating institution
>
> Lawton and Katsomitro, 2012

The OBHE report indicates that there are currently 200 degree-awarding IBCs in operation, with a number planned. The United Arab Emirates hosts the largest number, at 37, whilst the number in the People's Republic of

China has increased from 10 to 17. The USA, with 78 to its name, continues to provide the greatest number of IBCs, while the UK has 25, the second-largest number, with a further eight planned. However, in terms of total student numbers, Australian universities are prominent, with the US campuses having far smaller numbers (Lawton and Katsomitro, 2012). Humfrey (2013) suggests that western universities find it increasingly expensive in terms of time and resources to maintain their IBCs in Asia and the Far East and are beginning to pursue different models, such as partnership networks. The OBHE report (Lawton and Katsomitro, 2012) indicates that although IBCs will continue to be a minority pursuit compared to the volume of TNE activities more widely, they will nevertheless continue to grow as governments around the world see IBCs as an integral part of their educational aspirations.

Students who are registered at an IBC are unlikely to have any prior experience of the parent library service and unless a local, physical library presence is established, must rely totally on digital methods of access. This poses specific challenges for the parent library service and forms the focus of this chapter.

International engagement

According to Sweeney (2012) internationalization strategies are often driven by contemporary economic globalization and the need for income generation. For universities, internationalization may also imply a commitment to wider societal benefits. When university senior managers are engaged in devising international strategies, it is unlikely that library issues will be considered critical to the successful outcome of their discussions. Indeed, it is more common for university strategists to assume that digital access to library resources will be available and may be used as an incentive when negotiating agreements. Assumptions that digital access to resources will be seamless and require little support are also common. In both cases, this can lead to misunderstandings and difficulties for the library service once the details of new programmes are established. Even if library engagement is recognized as essential at a strategic level, once the actual planning for programme delivery is under way, library staff need to be proactive and persistent in delivering the message that the digital environment may not be the easy enabler it is assumed to be. Becker (2006), as a result of research undertaken at two Australian universities, makes this abundantly clear. She suggests that the library must provide a clear statement of its values, goals and objectives with respect to transnational educational issues, articulating where they fit into the university's vision, as well as devising a strategy for participating on committees working to internationalize the university. Ideally, a library-level memorandum of understanding should be established with the overseas campus and programme providers, articulating expectations and outlining any potential budget implications, such as the hidden costs of digital materials (Capita, 2012). In terms of funding, Becker recommends that the library must work towards establishing a stable budget for international activities and should find ways to tap into institutional funding for international practices. Squashing the myth that digital = free is of paramount importance at all levels of discussion.

Getting the basics right: IT infrastructure

It is often assumed by academic staff and students that digital access from anywhere in the world to the home library will be seamless, speedy and ultimately cost-neutral. There is rarely an expectation that operating digitally will incur extra expense. However, for a library to successfully support the delivery of digital services to an IBC, a range of additional resources and activities may need to be funded. In the first instance there is a need to establish a robust technical infrastructure which will support communication and resource discovery. Paul Greatrix (2012) makes the point that there are short windows for videoconferencing with IBCs at the other side of the world. This is true of all real-time communication methods. Services such as Skype and other online chat facilities can help with communication with students at a distance, but attention must be paid to time differences and local holidays. For locations such as South-east Asia making connections with the UK, for example, the time difference is 7 or 8 hours, meaning that it is almost the end of the working day in South-east Asia by the time staff are available in the UK. In practice, offline communications such as e-mail may prove more useful. Australian libraries working with South-east Asia do not have issues relating to synchronicity, but those working from US libraries have similar problems to those of the UK. The Brooklyn campus international library of Long Island University customized library services by setting up an active link connecting the library, Global College Headquarters and international sites in Costa Rica, China, India and Japan. Most of the library's resources and services are available around the clock. LivePerson software is used to enable students at international sites to chat with or send e-mails to a reference librarian (Wang and Tremblay, 2009).

Library staff on the home campus may take for granted a high level of local technical support and a fast network and may not appreciate some of the issues faced by staff and students based in an IBC. Local conditions, such as access to equipment or, indeed, consistent power supply, government policies and prior experience of technology all affect student expectations and expertise. Academic staff moving from the home campus will expect a similar level of provision to that which they have left, whereas academic staff employed directly in another country may have very different expectations. If there are problems with physical access to equipment or networking barriers such as speed and local firewalls, these can very quickly cause major issues for a digitally provided library service. If the problems are occurring several thousand miles away, in a country where the technical staff speak a different language and have no experience of the home library's environment, they can escalate and relying purely on digital communication is rarely sufficient. Ideally, library and IT staff should visit the partner campus (in both directions) so that they can experience at first hand any reported challenges and learn how the local infrastructure works. Local culture, accepted bureaucracies and ways of working can have a significant impact on access to technology and can be much more easily appreciated if they are experienced.

To illustrate the problems that can arise: Newcastle University in Singapore encountered issues relating particularly to e-book access. Many of the e-books relied on IP address recognition for access and from Singapore had to be directed through a remote application service (RAS). Users reported very slow download speeds and much frustration was focused on the library service as a result. To resolve this, the decision was made to adopt EZProxy as a means of direct access, resulting in a reduction of issues and improved speed of access.

Getting the basics right: copyright and licences

Expectations over the understanding of copyright issues in a digital environment may also vary significantly between library staff, academic staff and students and these issues can be magnified when dealing with an IBC. Attitudes to the moral and ethical issues surrounding copyright vary enormously in different countries and it cannot be assumed that staff and students based abroad will have the same understanding of the concept as home staff and students. Librarians should also be familiar with the local copyright law operating where the IBC is located. However, it is often unclear which country's copyright law takes precedence and how, at a distance, users can become digitally literate and understand their own and others' rights and responsibilities. For example, consider the scenario where a lecturer at an IBC wants to make a book chapter available to his students. The book is available in print in the home library, but it is not available digitally and is out of print, so cannot be easily purchased by the local IBC library. Will copyright law allow a digital copy of the chapter to be provided by the home library to the lecturer at the IBC? The copyright licence for UK universities implies that this is currently not possible, although the chapter could be made available if the course was running in the UK. This scenario illustrates the danger of making assumptions based on the permissions of the home country and the associated pretext of equitable access. It also highlights the problems which arise when the traditional approaches to the provision of print materials do not successfully migrate to the digital environment and as a result require librarians to consider alternative approaches to content provision.

Setting aside the technical and copyright issues, it might be expected that the digital world is the ideal environment for ensuring parity of access to resources and, indeed, at first glance this is the case. On closer examination it becomes clear that to ensure compliance, it is necessary to review licence agreements. Many licence agreements demonstrate that publishers and suppliers are keenly aware of the potential for maximizing their income by differentiating between different campuses and physical locations. This poses a variety of practical and ethical challenges for library staff. It is clearly imperative to abide within the law, but legal contracts are extremely complex and it is unlikely that academic librarians will have had the relevant experience or expertise to interpret the detail. In practice, successful outcomes are best achieved by close collaboration with university colleagues specializing in tenders and contracts. However, librarians need to be aware of the implications of licences and contracts for electronic resources which may be used by IBC students and need to be confident in their ability to initiate negotiations with publishers to ensure compliance.

Getting the basics right: access

An underpinning ethos of an international campus is that staff and students should enjoy parity of access with home students. It must also be recognized that it is not possible to predict with total accuracy what IBC students will need to access. In this context, there may still be discussions to be had about the feasibility of providing a gateway for IBC students which will restrict access to resources for which specific licence terms have been negotiated. This is a far from ideal solution in terms of parity of access, but, if technically possible, may go some way towards assuring legal compliance.

The Capita report (Capita, 2012) highlights the fact that the internet enables wider knowledge of locally based materials and states that a paradox of the digital age is the need to assure physical access. This is particularly relevant to students and staff based at a distance from their home library. Digital catalogues, databases and search engines raise awareness of print-only resources as well as digital materials not held by the home library. Within the home country, interlibrary loan services usually suffice to provide access to these materials, but for IBC users this may not be possible, or at least may come at an increased cost. Library staff also need time to learn about the in-country library facilities and how these might aid their students. Is there a national library, for example, and, if so, what kind of service might it provide? What other local library facilities are accessible? How do in-country interlibrary loans work? What are the prevailing norms for library use in the country? The digital library interfaces in the IBC country may not provide all its material in other languages, so that using purely digital means it is not always possible to answer these questions.

In addition, it is helpful to learn about the key in-country digital resources relating to the subject programmes. Using Singapore as an example again, we can provide digital resources relating to general marine engineering and UK facilities, but we may also need to know about Singaporean marine law and standards and to provide digital maps of the seas around Singapore rather than the UK.

On a pragmatic level therefore, it can be seen that providing parity of access to resources for IBC students is perhaps an unrealistic goal and that the emphasis needs to be on achieving a mix of local and digital resources scoped to provide as good a match as possible.

Getting the basics right: signposting support

The SCONUL report of 2008 (Senior et al., 2008) discussed issues of international students coming to the UK. In general, these students will be prepared for change. Students who stay in their own country and study at an IBC may not consider the need for any readjustment and may present a different attitude and approach to the library service delivered by the parent institution. They may have no direct personal contact and no physical experience to help them and their assessment of the service may be solely based on the digital environment provided by the library. It is essential, therefore, that the digital interface is of the highest quality.

The first challenge is to ensure that both staff and students at the IBC are aware of the resources and attendant support services available to them. Newcastle has addressed this by creating a digital library guide specifically for Singapore students, with subject pages which highlight key resources.[1] The guide also enables library staff to introduce themselves to the students, to explain how they can be contacted and to bring together links to the local libraries in Singapore alongside the Newcastle digital offering. Usage statistics demonstrate that it is well used and feedback from both academic staff and students indicate that it has been a useful resource:

> I just thought I'd thank you and colleagues for the time you put into setting-up the Singapore library guides; we found that there are various ways into some of the e-resources and without the guides we would have been in a bit of a mess here – students had no difficulties using these very quickly (so thanks very much!)   Programme Director, Singapore

Digital media such as video and online tutorials, for example those used by the University of Bolton at their Middle East campus, also demonstrate the advantage the digital environment provides for distance support.[2]

Supporting staff and students: blending face-to-face with the virtual

There are, however, issues with encouraging IBC students to communicate with the library. They may not be used to library staff offering help with assignments or with being able to ask for help in general. In a face-to-face situation, it is much easier to encourage students and explain to them that their questions are welcome. Digitally this can take a little more sustained effort and can involve having a regular presence, for example on Facebook or Twitter, or merely by sending regular e-mails to the whole cohort. Blending the virtual with the physical is also helpful. Students from the Singapore IBC, for example, visit Newcastle University each summer and this is an ideal opportunity for library staff to engage with them, making subsequent digital contact much more likely. Library staff run a series of workshops during the summer immersion programme, set information literacy assignments and attend as many of the social activities as possible, working to build up personal profiles to enable easier communication by e-mail in future. This approach has been partially successful; students who engaged via the informal e-portfolio blog during their visit were encouraged to share their experiences and photos of visiting the UK and those students who were most engaged are those who now communicate most frequently by e-mail if they need specific library help.

The Newcastle library team also found it helpful to create a digital welcome pack for academic staff in Singapore, explaining how the library can support their teaching and research and the services available for their students. However, experience indicates that including a face-to-face meeting is much more effective in building a long-term working relationship than relying purely on digital means. All new Singapore-based staff visit Newcastle for an induction programme in which the library participates, so they are able to see the base facilities and discuss any concerns they may have face-to-face. This also enables library staff to explain how to access library facilities and resources in Singapore. Nevertheless, there is rarely time to address more in-depth issues, such as information and digital literacy development of their students.

Supporting staff and students: information literacy

When developing information and digital literacy on the home campus, librarians are accustomed to working closely with their academic colleagues to embed concepts into the curriculum. Maintaining this kind of relationship with staff working at a distance can be challenging. In order to address this challenge, a module on Information for Learning for academic staff has also been developed in the virtual learning environment (VLE) (Bent, 2012). Based on material from the University's Certificate of Advanced Studies in Academic Practice, it introduces lecturers to the theories of information literacy as well as practical resources, such as ANCIL (Coonan and Secker, 2012) and Jorum (Jorum, 2012), which they can use to help them develop their teaching. Again, a face-to-face introduction to the virtual study material assists in its uptake; the digital resource as a standalone facility is much less successful.

As with home students, library staff also have a role in developing information-literate students and where there is a librarian in an IBC, it may be possible to integrate lectures and workshops into mainstream teaching.

However, integration into the curriculum has proven more difficult, as staffing levels can be low, with little or no opportunity to deliver on-site face-to-face tuition. At Newcastle, an alternative approach to support has been developed and is delivered online using the University's 'Information for Learning' module for Singapore students which is hosted in the VLE and covers a range of information literacy elements, such as designing search strategies, finding and evaluating sources and managing information ethically (Bent, 2012).

From an international perspective one aspect of information literacy which has commanded detailed attention is plagiarism. Extensive research (Carroll and Ryan, 2005a and 2005b) has highlighted the difficulties faced by international students coming to the UK, particularly from South-east Asia, in understanding western attitudes to plagiarism. These difficulties are magnified if the students remain in their home country and are less exposed to western understandings of the concept. Indeed, many academic and library staff in other parts of the world have very varying approaches to the subject of plagiarism themselves and, if they cannot agree, there is little hope that their students will develop the understanding that a western-based academic might wish. In an attempt to address the problem, the University of Bolton held a 'plagiarism week' at its international campus, where the staff and students got involved in a series of events designed to bring relevant plagiarism issues to the forefront. Another approach has been to use a plagiarism detection software, such as Turnitin. Its role can be twofold, as a developmental learning tool to enable students to understand how to write effectively without plagiarizing, as well as a vehicle for online submission of student assignments.

Staff development

Library staff need to develop a blend of cultural awareness underpinned by expertise in new technologies to enable them to offer a comprehensive package of support. Many libraries run 'understanding cultural difference' programmes for their staff to help them better support international students coming to the university. A slightly different kind of programme is needed to assist staff in liaising with an IBC. The team who are directly involved must be aware of the fine details of the culture and bureaucracy of the country in which the IBC is located to enable them to liaise successfully with their counterparts in any local libraries, as well as with the staff and students. For example, realizing that all Singaporean students live at home helped the Newcastle staff to better understand some of the students' expectations and pressures. As communication is mainly by electronic means, sensitivity to nuances of language and forms of address when sending e-mails, for example, is key to building up successful relationships. An understanding of the importance given to hierarchy within a Singaporean organization has also been helpful for Newcastle staff in teasing out some of the specifics of ordering books locally and this type of understanding is more easily achieved by a physical visit. Although much can be learned by 'second-hand' digital means, understanding is aided by library staff having the opportunity to visit the IBC to experience at first hand how everything works and to build personal contacts with key administrative and other support staff.

As has already been mentioned, a key staff development issue centres around developing expertise in legal issues surrounding copyright in different countries, contracts and licences, as well as developing a deeper understanding of how digital technology can be used to enhance the student experience. Library staff also need to be experts in a range of social media and confident in their use of online chat and videoconferencing facilities. They need to appreciate the difficulties that firewalls and local networks may pose. In order to develop digital teaching materials, they need to be confident in the use of virtual learning environments and able to develop online learning resources such as videos and podcasts.

Supporting library colleagues at an IBC

Consideration must also be given to any library staff who are physically located at the IBC. They may be staff directly employed by the home institution, in which case they are entitled to have access to any staff development opportunities provided to their colleagues. Can digital technology provide a means to bring them closer to their colleagues at 'home'? IBC library staff are often natives of the IBC country, with similar cultural variations from the home country to those of their students. Close attention must be given to their enculturation, to enable them to embody the same principles and practices and to adhere to the same quality standards as the home library. Regular communication, perhaps weekly via an online video chat facility, can help staff who may otherwise feel isolated to make links with other library colleagues; digital media has to be an essential part of their daily life. Wherever practicable, however, visits by such staff to the home library are recommended, as experience has shown that digital alternatives are no match for face-to-face experiences.

In other situations, the local library staff may owe their first allegiance to another organization or library and may not have the same sense of belonging to the distant library service. In this situation, the home library cannot exert any control over the IBC facilities and must be aware of local sensitivities and bureaucracies. However, opportunities for sharing and exchanging knowledge can be beneficial for all concerned and again, visits by library staff from both locations can help dispel misunderstandings and build closer working relationships more effectively than purely digital communication. Leong and Nguyen's study of continuing professional development of library staff in a multinational university emphasizes the need for a blended learning approach for staff development, encompassing both face-to-face and online components, concluding that a purely digital programme is less likely to be successful (Leong and Nguyen, 2011).

Becker (2006) also makes the point that effective library participation in transnational education must be led consistently, with clear goals and with opportunities for participation which are open to all, so that library staff at all levels are invested in the process. She suggests that a consistent source of funding will enable the library to be flexible and to respond rapidly to new initiatives, as well as enabling librarians to participate fully in any training or travel which is required. The latter point is often underestimated, but experience has shown that staff and student training sessions, ranging from culture to digital information literacy sources, given face-to-face in the international environment by home library staff, have greatly improved both knowledge and understanding and resulted in better working practices for both students and staff. A project undertaken by RMIT University in Melbourne with their Vietnam campus is a case in point. The primary focus 'was to assist the Vietnam library staff to meet their customers' service delivery expectations of a modern academic library' (Leong and Nguyen, 2011). RMIT's vast array of digital resources was not being utilized effectively by staff and hence students were losing some of the parity gained by having access to them. Following the blended learning training sessions, of which the online content included an online community of practice, many aspects of service were improved, as evidenced by both students and staff.

Conclusion

Given the large commitment of time, energy and expertise which library staff need to devote to transnational educational activities in general and especially those relating to IBCs, it is understandable that there is concern amongst library managers over the sustainability and funding for such activities. The additional, often hidden, costs of providing a largely digital offering need early attention. However, as detailed in Humfrey (2009) and more recently by the British Council (British Council, 2013), such development is inevitable and libraries can benefit from involvement. There are opportunities to raise their profile within their university and to demonstrate how fundamental a well organized digital library service is to a successful IBC initiative. By raising concerns at an early stage, funding for additional licences and digital resources can be factored into the planning process for any new initiative and a pre-prepared checklist of essentials for consideration is invaluable in initiating conversations with university strategists.

Involvement with transnational initiatives also provides a wonderful opportunity for staff development. Library staff have the opportunity to extend their horizons, perhaps to step outside their comfort zone or 'silo' and to learn about alternative library worlds. Liaising with and in some cases helping or being helped by library staff from other countries can also add interest and lead to increased motivation and job satisfaction, whether physically or virtually. However, it must be recognized that such changes from everyday activities can also lead to uncertainty, anxiety and work overload, so they must be planned and managed carefully.

One, perhaps unexpected, benefit of library engagement with transnational education, particularly in the digital environment, is the need to develop multi-professional teams with colleagues from across the organization. Library staff have to build strong working relationships with IT experts to ensure digital access to library resources from the IBC and likewise, links to academic and administrative staff are often more explicit and immediate. The benefits of team working are illustrated in a case study where staff from RMIT International University in Vietnam worked closely with staff of the Learning Skills and Educational Technology Units in preparing new lesson plans and training materials. As a result, the units now refer lecturers to the library when bespoke information literacy classes are required (Leong and Nguyen, 2011).

The library team at Newcastle now form part of a team comprising the Assistant Registrar, Teaching and Learning Dean, academic teaching staff, administrative and computing staff and representatives from the students' union, all working together to plan the summer immersion visit of the Singaporean students to Newcastle. Relationships developed within this environment often lead to better communication on other unrelated issues.

Does our digitally rich learning environment lead to unrealistic expectations of libraries in the transnational education environment? Perhaps it does, as many university strategists and indeed, library staff, may not be aware of all the underlying implications of providing a robust virtual library service to international campuses. It is inevitable, however, if such outposts are established, that libraries will need to engage with the process. If librarians are able to join institutional planning groups at an early stage, many of the underlying issues can be made clear and plans put into place to address them and to manage expectations to a realistic level. Concerns relating to funding, commitment of staff time and legal and ethical issues can also be aired and pragmatic solutions found. The opportunities afforded for library staff development, international networking and job satisfaction are a clear benefit, along with an enhanced library profile within the institution.

Notes

1   http://libguides.ncl.ac.uk/nuis.
2   www.bolton.ac.uk/library/Study-Skills/Home.aspx and
    http://data.bolton.ac.uk/bissto.

References

Becker, L. K. W. (2006) Globalisation and Internationalisation: models and patterns of change for Australian academic librarians, *Australian Academic and Research Libraries*, **37** (4), 282–98.

Bent, M. (2012) Developing Academic Literacies. In Secker, J. and Coonan, E. (eds), *Rethinking Information Literacy: a practical framework for teaching*, Facet Publishing, London.

British Council (2008) *A Review and Taxonomy: international college partnership models*, www.britishcouncil.org/a_review_and_taxonomy.pdf.

British Council (2013) *The Shape of Things to Come: higher education global trends and emerging opportunities to 2020*, Internationalising Higher Education, Hong Kong, http://ihe.britishcouncil.org/news/shape-things-come-higher-education-global-trends-and-emerging-opportunities-2020.

Capita (2012) *What Every University Librarian Needs to Know About Enhancing the Student Experience*, Birmingham, www.capita-fhe.co.uk/news/Pages/HEstudentexperiencewhitepaper.aspx.

Carroll, J. and Ryan, J. (2005a) Canaries in the Coalmine: international students in western universities. In Carroll, J. and Ryan, J. (eds), *Teaching International Students: improving learning for all*, Routledge, London and New York.

Carroll, J. and Ryan, J. (eds) (2005b) *Teaching International Students: improving learning for all*, Routledge, London and New York.

Coonan, E. and Secker, J. (2012) *A New Curriculum for Information Literacy (ANCIL)*, http://newcurriculum.wordpress.com.

Council of Europe (2002) *Code of Good Practice in the Provision of Transnational Education*, http://hub.coe.int/web/coe-portal.home.

Greatrix, P. (2012) The Real Bottom Line, *Times Higher Education*, 2 August, 26.

Humfrey, C. (2009) *Transnational Education and the Student Experience: a PMI student experience project report*, UKCISA, London.

Jorum (2012) *Jorum Repository of Learning and Teaching Materials*, www.jorum.ac.uk.

Lawton, W. and Katsomitro, A. (2012) *International Branch Campuses: data and developments*, Obervatory on Borderless Higher Education, www.obhe.ac.uk/documents/view_details?id=894.

Leong, J. and Nguyen, L. H. (2011) Continuing Professional Development for RMIT International University Vietnam Library Staff: adding value through an international partnership: a case study, *International Information & Library Review*, **43** (3), 169–75.

Senior, K., Bent, M., Scopes, M. and Sunuodula, M. (2008) *Library Services for International Students*, SCONUL, London, www.sconul.ac.uk/sites/default/files/documents/Libraryservicesforinternationalstudents-full.pdf.

Sweeney, S. (2012) *Going Mobile: internationalisation, mobility and the European Higher Education Area*, London, www.heacademy.ac.uk/assets/documents/internationalisation/Going_Mobile.pdf.

Wang, Z. and Tremblay, P. (2009) Going Global: providing library resources and services to international sites, *Journal of Library Administration*, **49** (1–2), 171–85.

Index

funders' requirements (*continued*)
Engineering and Physical
Sciences Research Council
(EPSRC) 88
research data management
(RDM) 88
future, Digital Tattoo project 116–18

Harvard University Open
Collections Program, Open
Educational Resources (OER)
76
Huddersfield University Library
activity data 141
recommendations 141

IBCs *see* international branch
campuses
infographics, Edge Hill University
55–7
information literacy
international branch campuses
(IBCs) 165–6
transnational education (TNE)
165–6
information management, Digital
Tattoo project 114
information storage, digital
marketing 15
innovation, recommendations 139
international branch campuses
(IBCs) 157–71
see also transnational education
(TNE)
access 162–3
copyright 161–2
coverage 158–9
defining 158
face-to-face support 164–5
information literacy 165–6
IT infrastructure 160–1
licences 161–2

Newcastle University/Singapore
157–71
Office for Borderless Higher
Education (OBHE) 158–9
signposting support 163–4
staff training and development
166–70
support services 163–6
time zone issues 160–1
international context
curation 87–8
research data management
(RDM) 87–8
international engagement,
transnational education (TNE)
159–60
IT infrastructure
international branch campuses
(IBCs) 160–1
transnational education (TNE)
160–1

Jisc (Joint Information Systems
Committee)
Developing Digital Literacies
programme 68–9
JiscLAMP project, activity data
152
Open Educational Resources
(OER) 66, 68–9
Scarlet project (Special
Collections using Augmented
Reality to enhance Learning
and Teaching) 76
SCONUL (Society of College,
National and University
Libraries) 68–9

key performance indicators (KPIs),
Edge Hill University 57–8

Lankes, David, digital marketing 3–5